Sweet as...

To Peter

First published in 2004 by New Holland Publishers (NZ) Ltd
Auckland • Sydney • London • Cape Town

218 Lake Road, Northcote, Auckland, New Zealand
14 Aquatic Drive, Frenchs Forest, NSW 2086, Australia
86–88 Edgware Road, London W2 2EA, United Kingdom
80 McKenzie Street, Cape Town 8001, South Africa

www.newhollandpublishers.co.nz

Publishing Manager: Renée Lang
Editor: Linda Cassells
Food Stylist: Alessandra Zecchini
Design: Rachel Kirkland at The Fount

Zecchini, Alessandra.
Sweet as …/easy to make desserts and baked treats/recipes by
Alessandra Zecchini; photographs by Shaun Cato-Symonds. 1st ed.
Includes index.

ISBN 1-86966-066-8

1. Desserts. 2. Pies. 3. Cake. I. Cato-Symonds, Shaun. II. Title.
641.86-dc 22

10 9 8 7 6 5 4 3 2 1

Colour reproduction by SC (Sang Choy) International Pte Ltd, Singapore
Printed by Kyodo Printing Co (Pte) Ltd, Singapore

Sweet as...

easy to make desserts and baked treats

Alessandra Zecchini

photography by Shaun Cato-Symonds

NEW HOLLAND

Fruit Vols au Vent - see recipe on page 85

Contents

Bread and Chocolate Tart - see recipe on page 11

Introduction

The sweetest things of life are best kept for last. They are a must for special moments, something to be shared, as well as selfish little indulgences. In this book I attempt to provide the reader with a broad range of everything sweet, from simple biscuits to sophisticated desserts – 102 recipes in total, including some great classics revisited for the home cook, some family treasures and many, many more new creations.

Of course not everyone is a 'dessert person'– why not is beyond me! But when it comes to desserts and sweet treats it is always better to keep the portions small. That way you won't overwhelm guests who don't have such a sweet tooth, and there's the added bonus of keeping the host or hostess happy – small portions halve the chances of an unfinished plate, and double the requests for second helpings.

Give some thought to what you serve to drink with these sweet treats. Only dessert wine or sweet liqueur should be served with desserts, as any other wine, even a special one, will suddenly taste acidic and bitter, so make sure your guests have emptied their glasses before slicing the cake. Coffee and tea, on the other hand, can accompany or follow most sweet things, with the exception of fruit and sorbets.

And as you know, all rules are made to be broken. Taste is a very individual matter, as well as a fashion statement. So don't follow these recipes too rigidly. They are also intended to inspire. Allow yourself to be creative and experiment with new ideas, after all, some of the most famous culinary creations were born out of accidents and mistakes.

Sweet regards
Alessandra Zecchini

Fresh Fruit and Mascarpone Crème Tart - see recipe on page 18

Tarts & Pies

Tarts and pies are the eternal desserts, comfort food and part of every family heritage. Who can't remember grandma's special pie?

There are lots of pastry variations in this section and even more fillings and toppings. Some are traditional with a few twists, some are completely innovative and all are delicious. But the best thing is that all the recipes are foolproof, so even if you don't believe you are a 'pastry person', or lack the time to roll out pastry, you can try my 'pressing down' method (see Erbazzone Dolce on page 16 or the Fresh Fruit Tart and Mascarpone Crème on page 18). This chapter is definitely one for the modern home cook.

BAKLAVA

My friend Eva taught me how to make my first baklava, and this is a variation of her original recipe. The quantities of sugar and butter may seem huge, but this recipe will satisfy many appetites and is perfect for parties of 20 people or more.

Ingredients

500g/1lb 2oz unsalted butter, melted
750g/1lb 10oz filo pastry
   (usually 2 packets)
100g/3½oz walnuts
1 cinnamon stick
200g/7oz almonds
200g/7oz hazelnuts
100g/3½oz sugar

SYRUP
500ml/17fl oz water
500g/1lb 2oz sugar
125ml/4fl oz honey
1 cinnamon stick
grated rind of 1 lemon
juice of ½ lemon

Makes approximately 60 pieces

Line a large baking tray with non-stick baking paper. Lightly brush the baking paper with the melted butter. Layer half of the filo (1 packet) on the tray, brushing every second sheet well with butter. In a food processor coarsely chop the walnuts with the cinnamon stick, then chop the almonds, then the hazelnuts. Mix the ground nuts and cinnamon together with the sugar and spread evenly over the prepared filo. Cover with the remaining filo sheets (the second packet), brushing every other sheet with butter. Pour the remaining butter over the top of the pastry. With a large knife cut the baklava into small rectangular or diamond shapes, no longer than 7cm (3 inches). Ensure you cut the pastry right down to the base, as it will be difficult to cut once the baklava is baked. Place in an oven preheated to 180°C (350°F) and bake for 1½ hours, until the top looks golden brown. To make the syrup, mix all the syrup ingredients in a heavy-based saucepan and bring to the boil. Simmer for 20–30 minutes, until the syrup starts to thicken. Pour the hot syrup over the hot baklava in 2 stages, making sure that all the pastry is well soaked. Serve cold and note that the baklava should be eaten within 3 days.

Tips and variations

Try adding unsalted pistachio nuts to the mixture. For a spicier version, add 5–10 cloves to the nut mixture.

BREAD AND CHOCOLATE TART

The richness of chocolate is balanced by the presence of bread, making the filling for this tart truly special. *(See photo on page 6)*

Ingredients

175g/6oz stale baguette bread
350 ml/11$\frac{1}{2}$fl oz milk
100g/3$\frac{1}{2}$oz dark chocolate
100g/3$\frac{1}{2}$oz unsalted butter
1 teaspoon vanilla or hazelnut essence
1 tablespoon cocoa
2 eggs
4 tablespoons sugar
250g/8oz frozen sweet short crust pastry
12 pecan nuts
whipped cream to serve (optional)

Serves 12

■ Tear the bread into small pieces in a bowl, cover with the milk and leave to soak. Melt the chocolate with the butter. Add to the bread and milk mixture and work with a wooden spoon to break up the lumps of bread, leaving a few small pieces for visual effect. Add the vanilla or hazelnut essence and the cocoa and mix well. In a separate bowl beat the eggs and sugar together until creamy, then fold into the bread mixture. Roll out the pastry to fill a 23cm (9 inch) round baking tin lined with non-stick baking paper or greased with butter and dusted with flour. Pour the filling into the pastry case and arrange the pecan nuts around the edge, with a nut for each slice. Bake in an oven preheated to 180°C (350°F) for approximately 35 minutes. Serve cold by itself or accompanied by whipped cream, if using.

Tips and variations

Substitute the pecan nuts with walnuts or almonds, or add a few chopped nuts to the filling mixture. For a sweeter tart, substitute the bread with savoiardi or sponge biscuits, using less milk and more biscuits. Add the milk gradually until the biscuits become soft.

CROSTATA DI FRUTTA - JAM TART

Crostata is the Italian name used for jam tarts, traditionally with a criss-cross pattern on top. This recipe makes a generous-sized tart that will keep for several days.

Ingredients

PASTRY
200g/7oz butter
150g/5oz sugar
3 eggs
450g/1lb flour (strong or plain)
2 teaspoons baking powder

FILLING
1 x 475g/1lb jar jam (any flavour)

Serves 12–14

■ To make the pastry cream the butter and sugar in a large bowl. Add the eggs one by one, then the flour and baking powder. Work into a soft dough, then immediately roll out three-quarters of the pastry and fill a 23cm (9 inch) round baking tin lined with non-stick baking paper or greased with butter and dusted with flour. Make sure the sides of the pastry shell are high enough to contain the filling. Spread the jam evenly over the pastry shell. Use the remaining pastry to make thin strips, and arrange them over the tart in a criss-cross pattern. Bake in an oven preheated to 180°C (350°F) for 25 minutes, or until a toothpick inserted in the tart comes out clean. Allow the tart to cool before serving.

Tips and variations

Red jams are best for colour, but apricot jam also gives great results. To make an easy apple pie, substitute the jam with apples, pre-cooked in a little sugar, lemon juice and cinnamon.

PLUM TART WITH SAMBUCA CRÈME

I live close to some beautiful plum orchards, which inspired me to create this tart. Sambuca is a sweet Italian aniseed liqueur.

Ingredients

PASTRY
150g/5oz flour (strong or plain)
½ teaspoon baking powder
50g/2oz butter, softened
75g/3oz sugar
1 egg yolk
1 tablespoon Sambuca liqueur
1 tablespoon warm water, plus
    1 tablespoon, if required

TOPPING
8 large plums, preferably Satsuma
    or Black Doris
icing sugar for dusting

SAMBUCA CRÈME
1 egg yolk
1 tablespoon sugar
1 tablespoon Sambuca liqueur
100ml/3½fl oz skimmed milk

Serves 8

To make the pastry mix the flour and baking powder with the softened butter, then add the sugar, egg yolk, Sambuca and water. Work into a dough. (It may be crumbly at first, but will form a dough with a little patience.) Add 1 tablespoon more water if necessary. On a lightly floured board roll out the pastry into a square, about 20 x 20cm (8 x 8 inches), cutting and pasting the pieces together until it makes a regular shape. As the piece gets bigger place it directly on an oven tray lined with non-stick baking paper and finish rolling there.

To make the tart cut the plums in half, remove the stones, and place the fruit cut side down on the pastry. For a 20 x 20cm (8 x 8 inch) base, arrange 4 plum halves down and 4 across the pastry, allowing 1 cm around the edge, which can be left flat. Place the tart in the centre of an oven preheated to 180°C (350°F) for approximately 20 minutes. Remove from the oven, dust with icing sugar and allow to cool on the tray.

To make the crème, half fill a medium saucepan with warm water and set over a medium heat. Whisk the egg yolk and sugar together in a small bowl, then add the Sambuca. Set the bowl over the saucepan of simmering water and continue to whisk the egg mixture, ensuring no water splashes into the bowl. Slowly add the milk and simmer, occasionally stirring until the mixture thickens. It should have the consistency of runny custard. Cool and set aside for serving.

To assemble, place a slice of tart with 2 halves of fruit on each plate, dust with more icing sugar, if desired (without clouding the glossy plum colour), and place 1 tablespoon of crème between the 2 plum halves.

Tips and variations

Although dark plums are best, you can use half dark and half yellow plums in a chequerboard pattern for visual effect. If the plum skins darken too much during baking, remove them while the plums are still hot to display the bright red flesh. The skins should come away easily.

FRUIT CIABATTA BREAD

This sweet ciabatta is easy to make even for the first-time bread baker. It adds a point of difference to your bread basket, goes well with butter, sweet preserves or cheese, and can be cut into small slices to serve like biscotti.

Ingredients

2½ teaspoons active dried yeast
1 teaspoon sugar
300ml/10fl oz warm water
300g/10½oz high-grade or strong flour, plus plenty for dusting
pinch of salt
pinch of cinnamon
2 tablespoons sultanas
1 tablespoon mixed citrus peel
icing sugar for dusting (optional)

Makes 2 medium loaves

In a large bowl dissolve the yeast and sugar in the warm water. Add the flour, salt and cinnamon and mix with one hand as this dough, unlike other bread doughs, is particularly sticky. Add the sultanas and citrus peel and mix well for 1–2 minutes. Place the dough on a generously dusted wooden board, cover the dough with more flour and then with a tea towel. Leave for up to 1 hour to rise, then remove the tea towel (it should not stick if you put enough flour on top of the dough), dust with more flour if necessary, and cut into two equal pieces with a large knife. Pick up each piece with both hands and place on a baking tray lined with non-stick baking paper, pulling the bread into its characteristic elongated ciabatta shape. Bake in an oven preheated to 220°C (410°F) for 20 minutes, then turn the loaves over and bake for a further 10 minutes. They are ready when the crust is crunchy. Sprinkle with icing sugar, if desired.

Tips and variations

To make a plain ciabatta bread, follow the same method, omitting the cinnamon and fruit. For a soft-crust chewy ciabatta, wrap the hot bread in a napkin, then place it in a plastic bag and seal. The steam from the hot bread will soften the crust, and will keep it fresh for 2–3 days.

MARSALA AND OLIVE OIL PASTRIES

A truly Mediterranean flavour for a little pastry that goes a long way. This recipe may inspire you to experiment more with olive oil.

Ingredients

200g/7oz self-raising flour
100g/3½oz sugar
100ml/3½fl oz olive oil
50ml/2fl oz Marsala wine
caster sugar for dusting

Serves many!

Mix the flour and sugar into a bowl, then add the olive oil and the Marsala. Mix well, first with a wooden spoon, then with your fingers, until it forms a soft dough. Line a 20cm (8 inch) round baking tin with non-stick baking paper and fill with the pastry, pressing it down with your fingers. Dust with caster sugar and bake in an oven preheated to 180°C (350°F) for 45 minutes. When cold, cut into very small slices and serve with coffee.

Tips and variations

Substitute Marsala with port or sherry. I like to use extra virgin olive oil for more flavour, but any olive oil will do. Olive oil is also a good alternative to butter in other pastries and bases, especially if you are trying to avoid dairy products.

PEAR AND GRAPPA PIE

This great recipe has been adapted from a wonderful book of Italian grappa recipes *La Grappa e i suoi Sapori (Grappa and its Flavours)*, by my friends Sandro Bottega and Giovanni Savio. For best results use firm rather than soft pears.

Ingredients

1kg/2lb 3oz pears
100g/3½oz unsalted butter
100g/3½oz sugar
100g/3½oz amaretti biscuits, crushed
150g/5oz apricot jam
2 tablespoons grappa
500g/1lb 2oz frozen sweet short
　　crust pastry
whipped cream to serve (optional)

Serves 12

Peel and core the pears and cut into thin slices. Melt the butter in a large saucepan. Add the pears and sugar and cook for 1–2 minutes, taking care not to allow the pears to disintegrate. Remove from the heat and add the crushed amaretti biscuits, apricot jam and grappa. On a lightly floured board roll out the pastry into two discs, one larger than the other. Use the larger one to fill a deep 23cm (9 inch) round pie dish lined with non-stick baking paper or greased with butter and dusted with flour. Spoon the pear mixture into the pie shell and cover with the other disc of pastry. Seal the edges and bake in an oven preheated to 180°C (350°F) for approximately 30 minutes. Serve warm or cold accompanied by whipped cream, if desired.

Tips and variations

Substitute the amaretti biscuits with savoiardi or sponge biscuits, and the pears with apples.

ERBAZZONE DOLCE

This sweet tart, which uses spinach as a base ingredient, is traditional in my part of Italy, Emilia Romagna. In my village everybody makes it, although no one shares their recipe to the full – some secrets must remain within the family! After several attempts, I too have devised my own erbazzone, and here is how I make it (no secrets!).

Ingredients

FILLING

300g/10$\frac{1}{2}$oz frozen spinach
300g/10$\frac{1}{2}$oz ricotta cheese
200g/7 oz sugar
100g/3$\frac{1}{2}$oz ground almonds
2 tablespoons Sambuca or Sassolino liqueur

PASTRY

150g/5oz unsalted butter
150g/5oz sugar, softened
3 egg yolks
2 tablespoons Sambuca or Sassolino liqueur
400g/14oz self-raising flour

ICING (optional)

2 tablespoons icing sugar
2 tablespoons Sambuca or Sassolino liqueur
water

Serves 12

To make the filling, defrost the spinach at room temperature, then squeeze out as much water as possible and mix with all the other filling ingredients.

To make the pastry, cream the butter and sugar together in a bowl, add the egg yolks and Sambuca or Sassolino, and then the flour and work into a soft dough. Line the base and sides of a 23cm (9 inch) round baking tin with non-stick baking paper and press three-quarters of the dough around the sides and base of the tin with your fingers. (This dough is too soft to roll.) Cover the pastry shell with the ricotta and spinach filling, then ease the edges of the pastry towards the centre of the pie. Make thin strips with the remaining pastry and arrange them in a criss-cross pattern over the pie. Place in the centre of an oven preheated to 180˚C (350˚F) for approximately 1 hour. Allow to cool.

To make the icing, mix the icing sugar with the liqueur, adding a few drops of water if it seems too hard, and spread over the criss-cross pastry pattern. Serve cold with coffee or a glass of sweet wine.

Tips and variations

Sassolino is a typical aniseed sweet liqueur from Emilia Romagna, used mainly for cakes, and it may be difficult to find elsewhere. Sambuca is more widely available and is a perfect substitute, although more expensive. The icing is not traditional, but I use it because everybody seems to like it! If you find this cake too 'green' decrease the amount of spinach and increase the amount of ground almonds.

FRESH FRUIT AND MASCARPONE CRÈME TART

This tart is so delicious you will want more! Classic looking, but with mascarpone rather than crème anglaise, colourful fresh fruit for topping and an easy-to-make almond pastry base. *(See photo on page 8)*

Ingredients

PASTRY
100g/3$\frac{1}{2}$oz unsalted butter
150g/5oz flour (strong or plain)
50g/2oz ground almonds
2 tablespoons sugar
pinch of salt
1 egg

FILLING
250g/9oz mascarpone
2 tablespoons Amaretto or other
    sweet liqueur
1 tablespoon icing sugar
fresh fruit to top (berries, stone fruit,
    tropical fruit)
1 tablespoon apricot jam to glaze
hot water

Serves 12

Cut the butter into small cubes and rub into the flour until it resembles fine breadcrumbs. Add the other dry ingredients, and finally the egg. Work into a soft dough, then shape into a ball. Wrap in cling film and refrigerate for 30 minutes. Line a 23cm (9 inch) round baking tin with non-stick baking paper, place the ball of pastry in the middle of the tin, then spread it out with your fingers until it covers the bottom and sides. (This pastry is too soft to roll.) Cover with more non-stick baking paper and fill with dried beans or baking weights. Bake the shell 'blind' in an oven preheated to 180°C (350°F) for approximately 10 minutes, then remove the beans or weights. Lower the heat to 140°C (300°F) and bake for a further 20 minutes. Allow to cool. To make the filling, mix the mascarpone with the liqueur and icing sugar and spread over the bottom of the cold tart shell. Top with plenty of fruit creating your pattern of choice, and making sure there are no large gaps between the pieces of fruit. This is easily done if you start with the bigger pieces, and then use the berries to fill the gaps. Heat the apricot jam with a little hot water and brush over the fruit to glaze. Refrigerate until serving time.

Tips and variations

This tart also looks stunning if you make it in a square or rectangular shape – create a chequerboard pattern for the former, and stripes for the latter, by using different fruit in a range of colours. Or you can use only one type of fruit, such as thinly sliced plums, seedless grapes, or cherries. If the glaze looks too opaque, brush a little liquid honey over the fruit before serving.

TORTA AI LAMPONI - RASPBERRY TART

This is one of my favourite creations!

Ingredients

PASTRY
100g/3½oz butter
100g/3½oz sugar
2 egg yolks
200g/7oz self-raising flour

FILLING
2 egg yolks
4 tablespoons sugar
200ml/7fl oz cream (single or double)
100g/3½oz savoiardi or sponge biscuits
  (alternatively use 100g/3½oz stale sponge)
1 tablespoon Amaretto liqueur (or another
  favourite liqueur)
100g/3½oz frozen raspberries

icing sugar for dusting

Serves 12

To prepare the base, cream the butter and the sugar together in a large bowl. Add the egg yolks, then the flour. Work into a soft dough, first with a wooden spoon and then by hand. Shape into a ball, wrap in cling film and refrigerate for 30 minutes. To prepare the filling, in another bowl beat the egg yolks together with the sugar until light and pale in colour. Add the cream and keep beating for 30 seconds. Crumble the savoiardi biscuits (or the sponge, if using) with your fingers and add to the egg and cream mixture. Add the liqueur and mix well, making sure that the biscuit pieces have fully absorbed the liquid. The mixture should come off the spoon in chunks, rather than run off. If the mixture is too runny, add a couple more biscuits. Press the pastry with your fingers into the base and sides of a 23cm (9 inch) round baking tin lined with non-stick baking paper, making sure that the sides are high enough to contain the filling. (This pastry is too soft to roll.) Spread the filling evenly over the base, then ease the sides of the pastry towards the centre of the tart. Place the frozen raspberries on top of the filling and gently press them down. They should be still visible on the top of the tart. Bake in an oven preheated to 180°C (350°F) for 45 minutes, or until a toothpick inserted in the centre comes out clean. Allow the tart to cool. Dust lightly with icing sugar before serving.

Tips and variations

Frozen blueberries, blackberries and other berry fruit can replace the raspberries. Fresh berries can also be used, but they may not hold their shape during baking.

DOLOMITE APPLE STRUDEL

This is the apple strudel my mother makes, the rustic croissant-shaped version typical of the Dolomite mountains in north-eastern Italy. It is a very simple pie, neither too sweet nor too buttery.

Ingredients

PASTRY
50g/2oz butter, cubed
200g/7oz high-grade or strong flour
2 teaspoons brown (or Moscovado) sugar
100ml/3½fl oz water

FILLING
juice of 1 lemon
4 teaspoons brown (or Moscovado) sugar
5–10 cloves, according to taste
1 cinnamon stick, broken into 2 pieces
1 tablespoon sultanas
1 tablespoon chopped walnuts
600g/1lb 5oz apples
Serves 8

Put the butter, flour and brown sugar into a bowl and mix. Add the water and work into a soft dough. Shape into a ball, wrap in cling film and place in the refrigerator. To make the filling, in another bowl mix together the lemon juice, brown sugar, cloves, cinnamon stick, sultanas and walnuts. Peel and cut the apples into the bowl with the lemon mixture. Roll out the pastry as thinly as possible into a large oval shape. Spread the fruit over the pastry and starting from the smallest end, fold the pastry over the fruit to make a large roll. Pinch both sides of the strudel to seal in the fruit, and turn them in to resemble a gigantic croissant. (The ends are usually discarded after baking, as they become too hard.) Gently place on a baking tray lined with non-stick baking paper, and bake in an oven preheated to 180°C (350°F), ideally fan, for approximately 1 hour. The strudel is ready when the crust looks cooked both on top and bottom. Serve hot or cold.

Tips and variations

Substitute sugar with honey and use wholemeal flour for a healthy-style dessert.

EASY-TO-IMPRESS PEACH AND APRICOT TART

I call this tart 'Easy-to-Impress' because it is quick and easy to make, yet sure to make a great impression on your guests. This recipe uses frozen pastry for convenience, but if you are a keen baker, use the pastry recipe for the Plum Tart *(page 12)*, substituting Sambuca liqueur with Amaretto.

Ingredients

5 peaches
5 apricots
250g/8oz frozen sweet short crust pastry
15g/½oz unsalted butter
5 teaspoons brown (or Moscovado) sugar
pistachio nuts to decorate (optional)

MASCARPONE CREAM
250g/9oz mascarpone
1 tablespoon icing sugar
2 tablespoons Amaretto liqueur

Serves 8

Halve the peaches and apricots, then peel and remove the stones. Roll out the pastry and fill a 23cm (9 inch) round baking tin lined with non-stick baking paper or greased with butter and dusted with flour. Arrange the peaches and apricots in a pattern, cut side down, leaving as little space as possible between the fruit. Cut the butter into small cubes and dot over the top, then sprinkle on the brown sugar and bake in an oven preheated to 180°C (350°F) for approximately 30 minutes. To make the cream, mix the mascarpone, icing sugar and Amaretto liqueur together in a bowl and refrigerate until serving time. This tart can be eaten warm or cold, decorated with chopped pistachio nuts, if desired, and accompanied by a generous helping of the Mascarpone Cream.

Tips and variations

It is better to use fresh fruit for this tart. Other stone fruit such as plums or cherries are suitable. Cooked or raw pears and apples are another option – just cut the fruit into slices rather than halves.

CHOCOLATE PASTRY WITH RICOTTA AND JAM FILLING

This is an easy recipe for a chocolate pastry that is also suitable for chocolate biscuits. For the filling, choose a thick fruit spread, possibly a low-sugar type, and some plain ricotta to balance the richness of the fruit.

Ingredients

PASTRY
100g/3½oz unsalted butter
150g/5oz sugar
1 egg yolk
1 tablespoon cocoa
200g/7oz flour (strong or plain)
water

FILLING
250g/9oz ricotta cheese
1 x 475g/1lb jar thick jam (apricot or
    raspberry) or marmalade
slivered almonds to decorate (optional)

Serves 12

Cream the butter and sugar in a large bowl. Add the egg yolk and cocoa and then the flour. Work into a soft dough, first with a wooden spoon and then by hand, adding a little cold water if necessary. Shape into a ball, wrap in cling film and leave to rest for 30 minutes in the refrigerator. Roll out the pastry to fill a 23cm (9 inch) round baking tin lined with non-stick baking paper or greased with butter and dusted with flour. Make sure the sides of the pastry shell are high enough to contain the filling. Next bake the pastry shell. Place a sheet of non-stick baking paper filled with dried beans or baking weights on top of the pastry base and bake the shell 'blind' in an oven preheated to 180°C (350°F) for 10 minutes. Remove the paper and beans or weights and allow the shell to cool slightly. Spread the ricotta and then the jam or fruit spread over the pastry base, decorating the top with slivered almonds, if desired. Bake at 180°C (350°F) for 20 minutes or until a toothpick inserted in the pastry comes out clean. Allow the tart to cool and the jam to set before serving.

Tips and variations

To make a two colour tart, fill half the shell with apricot jam and the other half with raspberry jam. They both go incredibly well with chocolate. You can also fill this tart with fresh or canned apricots, then top it with a thin layer of apricot jam.

TORTA AL RABARBARO - RHUBARB TART

I'd like to dedicate this recipe to the great New Zealand writer Dick Scott, who loves rhubarb tart (and heartily approved of this one). You may find you have some extra syrup left over, and if so, simply store for later use.

Ingredients

PASTRY
100g/3½oz butter
100g/3½oz sugar
2 egg yolks
200g/7oz self-raising flour

FILLING
1kg/2lb 3oz rhubarb
250ml/8½fl oz water
1 teaspoon lemon juice
250g/9oz sugar

whipped cream or mascarpone to serve

Serves 12

To make the pastry, cream the butter and sugar together in a large bowl. Add the egg yolks, then the flour. Work into a soft dough, then shape into a ball, wrap in cling film, then refrigerate for 30 minutes. To prepare the filling, clean the rhubarb, discarding the ends of the stalks, and cut into 5cm (2 inch) pieces. In a medium-large saucepan bring the water to the boil with the lemon juice and half the sugar. Add the rhubarb, watching closely so that it cooks but does not disintegrate. As soon as white foam starts to appear (after approximately 2 minutes) remove from the heat and drain through a colander, reserving the liquid in another saucepan. Return the liquid to the heat, add the remaining sugar and simmer for 15–25 minutes until the liquid has reduced to a thick syrup. Roll out the pastry to fill a 23cm (9 inch) round baking tin lined with non-stick baking paper or greased with butter and dusted with flour. Make sure that the sides of the pastry are high enough to contain the filling. Spread the rhubarb evenly over the base of the pastry shell, then slowly pour over the syrup, taking care not to overfill the shell. Ease the edges of the pastry towards the centre of the pie. Bake in an oven preheated to 180°C (350°F) for 45 minutes, or until a toothpick inserted in the edge of the pastry comes out clean. Allow to cool before serving on its own or with whipped cream or mascarpone.

Tips and variations

This tart can be served by itself or with Sambuca crème (see Plum Tart with Sambuca Crème, page 12). Add any remaining syrup to some whipped cream or mascarpone to serve with the tart. The syrup can also be used to make jelly, to colour and flavour icing and meringues, as the juice of an unusual fruit salad, to make ice blocks, and even as a cordial for drinks and herbal teas. Substitute half the rhubarb with cooking apples to make a different flavoured tart.

Sacher Torte - see recipe on page 44

Cakes & Gateaux

The pièce de résistance of all desserts, a cake or gateau always makes a statement. It is the symbol of birthdays, weddings and all special occasions. Cakes can be rich and luscious, or light and delicate, or nutty, simple, extravagant, and they come in all sizes. I am particularly passionate about inventing new cakes, as well as revisiting old recipes devised before commercial baking powder became the norm. The result is a chapter full of ideas and delicious cakes, to make your next special occasion a triumph.

BANANA AND MAPLE SYRUP CAKE

Banana cakes are usually made just to use up over-ripe bananas and also seem to carry a healthy image. So this is the perfect chance to bake something for that health-conscious friend (or friends), using wholemeal flour and no dairy products. It will be appreciated.

Ingredients

400g/14oz ripe bananas
2 eggs
100g/3½oz sugar
1 teaspoon vanilla essence
50ml/2fl oz vegetable oil
200g/7oz wholemeal (whole wheat) flour
1 teaspoon baking powder
5 tablespoons maple syrup
whipped cream or ice-cream to serve

Serves 10

■ Line the base and sides of a 20cm (8 inch) round baking tin with non-stick baking paper. Peel the bananas and mash with a fork in a bowl. Add the eggs, sugar, vanilla essence and oil and mix with an electric beater. While beating, add the flour and baking powder. Pour the mixture into the baking tin and bake in an oven preheated to 180°C (350°F) for 40 minutes or until a toothpick inserted into the centre of the cake comes out clean. Make little holes on the top of the cake with the toothpick, then slowly pour the maple syrup on top, 1 tablespoon at a time, covering the whole surface. Serve cold with whipped cream or ice-cream.

Tips and variations

Sultanas and walnuts can be added to the mixture for a richer cake. Substitute maple syrup with golden syrup, or use an Amaretto liqueur caramel, as in the recipe for Amaretto Flan with Apricots and Amaretto Caramel (page 45).

CAFFELATTE PLUM CAKE

This is the perfect plum cake for a Continental breakfast or mid-afternoon coffee. Straight out of the oven it smells just like a bowl of caffelatte, but if you have to eat it cold, dunk it in your coffee!

Ingredients

150g/5½oz butter, melted
200g/7oz sugar
3 eggs
400g/14oz self-raising flour
1–2 drops vanilla essence
150ml/5½fl oz milk
150ml/5½fl oz strong espresso coffee

Serves 10–12

■ Whisk the melted butter and sugar together with an electric beater. Add the eggs, half of the flour and all the vanilla essence. Divide the mixture equally into 2 bowls. To one mixture add the milk, then half of the remaining flour, beating continuously. To the other mixture add the coffee and the rest of the flour. (If you follow this order you will not need to rinse the beater blades.) Line the base and sides of a 23 x 13cm (9 x 5 inch) loaf tin with non-stick baking paper. Pour in half of the milk mixture, then cover with half of the coffee mixture, and repeat until the tin is full. Bake in an oven preheated to 180°C (350°F) for approximately 40 minutes or until a toothpick inserted into the centre of the cake comes out clean. Allow the cake to cool in the tin, then lift it out of the tin with the baking paper. Remove the paper and serve with tea or coffee.

Tips and variations

This cake will still be good after a few days. Toast slices of the cake when it hardens and spread with butter. Use hot cocoa instead of coffee, or add a bit of cinnamon to the dark mixture.

BAKED CHEESECAKE

This is my easiest cheesecake recipe, well suited to a great number of variations. I make it with either 1 or 2 pots of cream cheese, the first lighter and more suited to fruit topping, the second richer and reminiscent of traditional Jewish cheesecakes.

Ingredients

BASE
100g/3½oz flour (plain or strong)
50g/2oz sugar
50g/2oz butter
1 egg
grated zest of ½ lemon

FILLING
Either 250g/8oz or 500g/1lb cream cheese
1 x 395g (13oz) can sweetened
    condensed milk
3 eggs
4 tablespoons lemon juice
grated zest of ½ lemon

TOPPING (optional)
2 tablespoons sugar
grated zest of 1 lemon

Serves 12

■ To prepare the base, mix the flour with the sugar and butter, then add the egg and lemon zest and work into a dough. Line the base and sides of a 20cm (8 inch) round baking tin with non-stick baking paper. If you use the double quantity of cream cheese you will need a 23cm (9 inch) baking tin. Place the dough in the centre of the baking tin and spread it over the base of the tin with your fingers. (This pastry is too soft to roll.) To make the filling, mix all the ingredients together, either in a food processor or with an electric beater, then pour over the base. Bake in an oven preheated to 160°C (325°F) for 1 hour. To make the optional topping, mix the sugar with the lemon zest. Sprinkle over the top and bake for a further 5 minutes. Switch off the oven and allow the cake to cool in the oven. Serve cold the next day.

Tips and variations

The richer cheesecake should be served on its own with tea or coffee rather than after a meal. The lighter version can be offered as a dessert, topped with fresh berries.

CHERRY BERRY AND YOGHURT CAKE

When I was developing this recipe I couldn't decide if it tasted better with cherries or with berries, so I ended up using a mixture of both.

Ingredients

150g/5oz butter
200g/7oz sugar
4 eggs
250g/8½oz self-raising flour
grated rind of 1 lemon
100g/3½oz mixture of fresh cherries,
    stoned, and frozen berries

TOPPING
2 tablespoons Greek-style yoghurt
2 tablespoons sugar
icing sugar for dusting
fresh cherries and berry fruit to serve

Serves 12

Line the base and sides of a 23cm (9 inch) round baking tin with non-stick baking paper. Melt the butter and whisk with the sugar, using an electric beater. Add the eggs, the self-raising flour, and the lemon rind. Pour into the tin. Place the cherries and/or berries on top. To make the topping, mix the yoghurt with the sugar, and pour over the cake making a circular pattern in the centre. (This quantity won't cover the cake completely.) Bake in an oven preheated to 180°C (350°F) for approximately 45 minutes or until a toothpick inserted into the centre of the cake comes out clean. Allow the cake to cool in the tin, then lift out with the baking paper. Remove the paper, dust with icing sugar and serve by itself or accompanied by more yoghurt and fresh cherries and berries.

Tips and variations

For a surprise taste put fresh basil leaves under the yoghurt topping (not on top as they will burn). This recipe is also suitable for a delicate apple or peach cake. Just peel and thinly slice your choice of fruit and, instead of placing it on top, fold the sliced fruit into the cake mixture. But be careful not to use more than 100g/3½oz of fruit, or it will become too heavy and sink to the bottom.

CRÊPE GATEAU

This is one of my mother's unusual cakes which I always loved as a child because it was so unique, both in taste and in texture.

Ingredients

CRÊPES
250g/8½oz plain flour
500ml/1 pint milk
4 eggs
50g/2oz butter

FILLING
100g /3½oz unsalted butter
5 tablespoons sugar
3 tablespoons Cointreau, Grand Marnier or
   other citrus liqueur (optional)

fresh berry fruit to serve

Serves 12

Mix the flour with half the milk until there are no lumps, then add all the eggs. Continue whisking, then add the rest of the milk. Cover the batter and leave to stand for 1 hour. (This batter should make about 25–30 very thin crêpes, but fewer, thicker crêpes can also be used.) Melt the butter in a 20cm (8 inch) non-stick frying pan. Pour the melted butter into the crêpe batter and stir well. (Adding the butter now means there is no need to grease the frying pan before making each crêpe.) Pour about half a ladle of batter into the medium-hot frying pan, and spread evenly to cover the base to the edges. When the edges of the crêpe start to curl up it is ready to turn over. Stack the finished crêpes one on top of the other and allow them to cool. To make the filling, cut the cold unsalted butter into small cubes. Place in a small mixing bowl, add 4 tablespoons of the sugar, and work into a soft cream with a wooden spoon. (Do not melt the butter, as it does not work in the same way.) Add the remaining sugar and the Cointreau, and work for a few more minutes. Place the first crêpe onto a serving plate, spread over some butter and cover with a second crêpe. Continue this way until all the crêpes are stacked, spreading the remaining butter around the edges and top of the cake. Refrigerate until 30 minutes before serving. This cake is filling, so serve only thin slices, possibly with fresh berry fruit, marinated in Cointreau or other liqueur, if desired.

Tips and variations

A good crêpe is thin and not too pale, with the occasional brown mark here and there. Use the juice of an orange or a lemon instead of Cointreau for a liqueur-free dessert. If the cake appears too dry, more juice and liqueur can be poured over the top. Flambé the cake with warmed liqueur at the table to produce a dramatic effect, but make sure you use a special hotplate for the crêpes.

SOFT HAZELNUT CAKE

Only the best hazelnuts will do, preferably organic and roasted. If you cannot find roasted nuts, place them in a hot oven for a minute or two, then into a clean tea towel to remove the skins.

Ingredients

100g/3½oz hazelnuts
3 eggs, separated
300g/10½oz sugar
100g/3½oz unsalted butter
200g/7oz flour (plain, high-grade or strong)
100ml/3½fl oz milk
1 tablespoon Frangelico (optional)

TOPPING
2 tablespoons hazelnuts
1 tablespoon sugar
2 tablespoons Frangelico liqueur (or
    other liqueur)
icing sugar for dusting

Serves 10–12

Finely grind the hazelnuts in a food processor. (Don't overdo or they will turn into a buttery paste). Mix the egg yolks together with the sugar and butter, add the ground hazelnuts, then the flour. Thin the mixture down with the milk and Frangelico. Beat the egg whites into stiff peaks, then fold into the mixture. Line the base and sides of a 23cm (9 inch) round tin with non-stick baking paper, and pour in the mixture. Bake in an oven preheated to 160°C (325°F) for approximately 30 minutes. Cover the cake with tinfoil to prevent the top from burning, and bake for a further 20 minutes or until a toothpick inserted into the cake comes out clean. To prepare the topping, grind the hazelnuts and sugar together, then add the Frangelico. Spread the hazelnut paste over the top of the warm cake and dust with icing sugar. Turn the oven off and return the cake to the oven to dry, preferably overnight. Cut when cold and serve with tea or coffee.

Tips and variations

Serve only small slices, as this cake is quite sweet and rich. If Frangelico is not available, use hazelnut essence instead. For an almond or walnut cake, follow the same recipe, substituting the nuts.

CHOCOLATE MERINGUE GATEAU

This is a variation of the traditional New Zealand pavlova, with an attractive, chocolate-dotted 'Dalmatian' look, and fresh cherries on top. Make this cake the evening before you serve it so it can be left in the oven overnight.

Ingredients

50g/2oz dark chocolate, grated & chilled
4 egg whites
pinch of salt
½ teaspoon cream of tartar
300g/10½oz caster sugar
1 teaspoon lemon juice

TOPPING
300ml/10 fl oz whipping cream
50g/2oz dark chocolate
20 fresh cherries

Serves 8–10

Beat the egg whites with the salt and cream of tartar into stiff peaks. Continue beating and add the sugar, 1 tablespoon at a time. Fold in the lemon juice, then the grated chocolate. Spoon the mixture over a baking tray lined with non-stick baking paper. Pile the meringue about 8 centimetres (3 inches) high, making a round shape but without pressing the mixture down too much. Place in the centre of an oven preheated to 180°C (350°F). Turn the oven off immediately and leave overnight, taking care not to open the oven door during this time. To prepare the topping, whip the cream, then grate the chocolate and, reserving 1 tablespoon for serving, fold in with the cream. Cover the meringue with the cream, sprinkle the remaining grated chocolate on top, and decorate with the cherries.

Tips and variations

Whip the cream with 2 tablespoons of icing sugar and 1 tablespoon of cocoa. Top with raspberries or other berries, but always use fresh fruit.

COINTREAU RICE CAKE

This is a lovely and unusual cake, especially for those who like rice and risotto, but are not too keen on hot rice pudding. I experimented with several types of liqueur here, until my husband (who has tasted everything in this book) suggested Cointreau, which works beautifully.

Ingredients

200g/7oz arborio or short grain risotto rice
250ml/8½fl oz water
4 tablespoons Cointreau liqueur
250ml/8½fl oz milk
150g/5oz sugar
200ml/7fl oz single cream
50g/2oz ground almonds
2 eggs

SYRUP
4 tablespoons water
1–2 tablespoons sugar
2 tablespoons Cointreau liqueur

Serves 12

Put the rice in a pot and cover with the water and 2 tablespoons of the Cointreau. Leave for 30 minutes, then add the milk and half the sugar and bring to the boil. Watch the pot carefully, as the milk tends to boil over. Simmer the rice until it is soft and almost all the liquid has been absorbed – it should look like a risotto. Pour into a mixing bowl, and fold in the remaining Cointreau and sugar, the cream, ground almonds and eggs. Line the base of a 23cm (9 inch) round baking tin with non-stick baking paper, grease well with butter and flour the sides of the tin. Pour the mixture into the tin and bake in an oven preheated to 180°C (350°F) for 35–40 minutes or until a toothpick inserted into the cake comes out clean. Allow the cake to cool inside the baking tin, then turn it out onto a plate (if you do this while the cake is still hot, it will break). To make the syrup, mix the water, sugar and Cointreau together in a saucepan and bring to the boil, stirring until the sugar has dissolved, then pour over the cake. Serve cold – it is actually better the next day.

Tips and variations

Add a little lemon zest or orange zest to the cake mixture or to the syrup. Make a greater quantity of syrup with 250ml (8½fl oz) water, 2 tablespoons Cointreau, and 6 tablespoons sugar, and pour over each slice when serving. For a completely different taste, substitute Cointreau with Sambuca or Amaretto.

PANETTONE WITH RICOTTA FILLING

Panettone is a traditional Italian Christmas cake, available in many delicatessen stores. It is delicious by itself, but more so if filled with sweet crèmes. This recipe is extremely easy, takes little time to prepare and creates a great effect. Every year I try something different, but this ricotta filling is probably one of the best.

Ingredients

250g/8¹⁄₂oz soft ricotta cheese
1 tablespoon icing sugar
1 tablespoon plus 5 teaspoons
    Amaretto liqueur
50g/2oz dark chocolate
5 amaretti biscuits
1 1kg/2lb 3oz panettone
200ml/7fl oz whipping cream

Serves 12

In a bowl mix the ricotta and icing sugar together with 1 tablespoon of the Amaretto liqueur. Chop the chocolate into small pieces with a knife and fold into the ricotta mixture. Crush the amaretti biscuits with your fingers over the ricotta and fold in. Open the panettone box and keep the plastic wrapping for later use. Cut the top off the panettone and, using a small knife, cut around the inside of the cake, leaving 3cm (1 inch) along the sides and bottom. Scoop out the inside of the cake with your fingers, taking care not to break the panettone shell. Crumble the pieces of panettone over the ricotta filling and fold in. Whip the cream until very stiff. Add the cream to the ricotta mixture and fold in lightly. Brush the top and inside of the panettone shell with the remaining Amaretto liqueur. Fill the shell with the ricotta mixture and place the panettone lid on top. Put the panettone back in its plastic bag, close and refrigerate for at least 6 hours, preferably overnight. To serve, bring the whole cake to the table on a serving plate and slice on request. It is beautiful on its own, or accompanied by a crème anglaise.

Tips and variations

A soft ricotta is needed for this recipe; if your ricotta is too hard, soften it with a wooden spoon and a couple of teaspoons of cream or milk. Chocolate is easier to chop or grate if it has been stored in the refrigerator. Substitute the ricotta with mascarpone for a richer texture. Instead of amaretti biscuits try candied orange peel or a mixture of toasted and crushed hazelnuts and pistachio nuts. If you don't have Amaretto, use any other sweet liqueur, and for a stronger-tasting version try rum or brandy. For a richer filling use 2 eggs and 200ml (7fl oz) cream and follow the method in Tiramisù di Alessandra (page 68). This version will need to be refrigerated overnight.

PANFORTE DI SIENA

The Tuscan bakeries that make this famous cake have their recipes patented, so it is impossible to reproduce it exactly as it is commercially made. The availability of ingredients can also be a factor – Italian almonds and citrus peel have quite a distinctive taste, and traditional panforte contains candied melon and acacia honey, which are hard to find. This version, made with ingredients available outside Italy, is easy to follow, and the result quite professional.

Ingredients

2 tablespoons honey
2 tablespoons vanilla-flavoured sugar
2 tablespoons, icing sugar, plus more
    for dusting
1–2 tablespoons water, if required
150g/5½oz citrus peel
200g/7oz candied papaya
150g/5½oz almonds (blanched)
100g/3½ oz plain flour
1 teaspoon powdered coriander
1 teaspoon powdered cinnamon
¼ teaspoon powdered nutmeg

Serves 10–12

■ Partly fill a small saucepan with hot water and set over a medium heat. In a bowl put the honey, vanilla sugar and icing sugar with 1–2 tablespoons water, depending on the thickness of the honey. Set the bowl over the pan of simmering water and stir the honey until runny. Remove the bowl from the heat and add the citrus peel, papaya, almonds and all the other dry ingredients. Line the base and sides of a 20cm (8 inch) round baking tin with non-stick baking paper. Fill the tin with the mixture, cover with another sheet of baking paper, and gently press down the cake evenly in the tin. Bake in an oven preheated to 160°C (325°F) for 25 minutes, then remove the top sheet of baking paper and bake for a further 20 minutes or until ready. Remove from the oven but leave in the baking tin and cover with a thick layer of icing sugar. Serve cold in small slices as it is quite filling.

Tips and variations

Traditional panforte is pressed and baked between 2 *ostie* (thin, rice paper-like sheets). These are difficult to find, but if available, use instead of baking paper and do not remove the *ostie* after baking. The vanilla-flavoured sugar is simply white sugar kept in a sealed jar with a vanilla pod in it. If acacia honey is not available, experiment with any local variety, such as clover honey. It is remarkable how this one ingredient can influence the taste of the cake. Panforte is ideal for Christmas and for gift-giving at other times, as it will last several weeks in an airtight container.

MILLE-FEUILLE

A sophisticated and formal dessert that has many variations. This recipe is very easy to follow, using frozen puff pasty to save time, and a basic crème for the filling.

Ingredients

PASTRY
300g/10½oz frozen puff pastry (2 sheets)
water to brush
icing sugar to dust

FILLING
2 eggs
3 tablespoons sugar
1 tablespoon plain flour
500ml/1 pint milk
1 vanilla pod
15g/½oz butter
300ml/10½fl oz whipping cream
liqueur to brush (optional)

icing sugar for dusting

Serves 12

Defrost the puff pastry and roll into two equal squares measuring approximately 25cm (10 inches). Make small incisions on the pastry with a fork, so it will rise evenly, then brush with water and sprinkle with icing sugar. Bake in an oven preheated to 180°C (350°F) for 10 minutes or until golden on top. Cool completely, then cut horizontally across each piece of pastry, where it naturally divides, making 2 thin sheets. Set aside the 4 sheets, keeping the best-looking, most golden one for the top. To make the filling, mix the eggs with the sugar and flour in a medium saucepan, then add the milk and vanilla pod and bring to the boil. Cook until creamy, then add the butter and allow to cool, stirring occasionally. In a bowl whip the cream until stiff. Remove the vanilla pod from the cold custard, then carefully fold in the whipped cream, a spoonful at a time. Place the thickest pastry base on a serving dish and brush with liqueur, if desired. Add one third of the crème, cover with another sheet of pastry, and continue this way, finishing with the fourth pastry sheet. Dust generously with icing sugar and refrigerate for at least 3–4 hours, preferably overnight, until serving time. Slice and serve by itself or with fresh berries.

Tips and variations
Ready rolled pastry is easier to use and saves time. Alternate vanilla crème and chocolate crème layers. Add coffee, liqueur, chestnut purée or fruit to the crème. Serve with a coulis made by blending berries and sugar, or passionfruit pulp. The mille-feuille can also be cut into small squares.

YEAST CAKE

This delicious cake is made using active dried yeast, giving it the aroma and texture of a sweet soft bread.

Ingredients

120ml/4fl oz milk
2 teaspoons active dried yeast
4 tablespoons caster sugar
50g/2oz butter, melted
250g/8½oz strong or high-grade flour
1 teaspoon vanilla essence
3 eggs
1 tablespoon sultanas
1 tablespoon mixed citrus peel

GLAZE
1 teaspoon apricot jam
water
pumpkin seeds and/or slivered almonds
   to decorate

Serves 12

Gently warm the milk in a saucepan, then transfer to a bowl. Dissolve the yeast and a pinch of the caster sugar in the warm milk. Allow to stand for a few minutes until it becomes frothy. In a large bowl mix together the melted butter, flour, sugar, vanilla essence and yeast liquid. Add the eggs and beat well, preferably with an electric beater. Fold in the sultanas and citrus peel. Line the base and sides of a 20cm (8 inch) round baking tin with non-stick baking paper and pour in the mixture. Cover with a large bowl (not a cloth) and allow to rise at room temperature until double in size (about 1 hour). Bake in an oven preheated to 180°C (350°F) for 15 minutes, then cover with tin foil and bake for a further 15–20 minutes or until a toothpick inserted in the cake comes out clean. To prepare the glaze, dilute the apricot jam with a little hot water. Brush the glaze over the top of the cake when cooked, sprinkle over a few pumpkin seeds and slivered almonds, and return the cake to the oven for a further 5 minutes. Serve warm or cold with a cup of coffee or tea, or with a glass of sparkling sweet wine.

Tips and variations

Possible toppings include poppy, sunflower and sesame seeds, dried or glacé fruit, and a variety of nuts.

GENOESE SPONGE

The Genoese is a common Italian sponge used by many pastry chefs as the base of more elaborate cakes, but it is also delicious on its own, covered with icing sugar, to accompany a cup of coffee.

Ingredients

5 eggs, separated
140g/5oz sugar
grated lemon zest
120g/4oz flour (plain or high-grade)
50g/2oz butter, melted
icing sugar for dusting (optional)

Serves 10–12

Partly fill a small saucepan with hot water and set over a medium heat. Set a bowl over the simmering water and whisk the egg yolks together with the sugar, turning in the same direction, until they are light and foamy. Remove from the stove and add the lemon zest, then the flour, gradually, and finally the melted butter. Beat the egg whites into stiff peaks and fold into mixture. Line the base of a 23cm (9 inch) round baking tin with non-stick baking paper, then grease and flour the sides of the tin. Pour the mixture into the tin and bake in an oven preheated to 180°C (350°F) for 25–30 minutes or until a toothpick inserted into the sponge comes out clean. Cut only when cold and serve dusted with icing sugar, if desired.

Tips and variations

Replace the lemon zest with orange zest, or vanilla essence, or liqueur. For a chocolate sponge add 1 tablespoon of cocoa with the flour.

POTATO FLOUR SPONGE

Potato flour, mixed with plain flour, is commonly used in European patisserie to give lightness to many cakes and sponges. This sponge is foolproof, as long as you take your time to fold in all the ingredients carefully.

Ingredients

4 eggs, separated
200g/7oz sugar
200g/7oz unsalted butter, melted
100g/3½oz plain flour
100g/3½oz potato flour
1½ teaspoons baking powder
1 teaspoon vanilla essence
pinch of salt
icing sugar for dusting (optional)

Serves 12

In a large mixing bowl beat the egg yolks with the sugar for a few minutes with an electric beater. Add the melted butter and keep beating until soft and airy. In a separate bowl sift the two flours and the baking powder together and add half to the egg mixture, folding in with a spatula or wooden spoon (never use an electric beater at this stage). Press out any lumps against the side of the bowl. Add the rest of the flour and fold in, then add the vanilla essence and a pinch of salt. Beat the egg whites into stiff peaks and fold into the mixture, half at a time. Cover the base of a 23cm (9 inch) round baking tin with non-stick baking paper, then grease and flour the sides of the tin. Pour the mixture into the tin and bake in an oven preheated to 180°C (350°F) for 35–40 minutes or until a toothpick inserted into the cake comes out clean. Cut only when cold and serve dusted with icing sugar, if desired.

Tips and variations

Replace the vanilla essence with the zest of 1 lemon. Fill and/or top with jam, cream, chocolate, fresh fruit or even ice-cream. This cake is extremely versatile.

TORTA ANTICA

I love to collect old recipes – this one came from a barely legible but beautifully handwritten manuscript, over 100 years old, from the north Italian city of Feltre. The recipe, possibly much older than its record, has been attributed to the kitchen of one of the city's noble families, and it starts like this: 'Take 24 eggs, and beat the yolks with half a measure of sugar for one hour . . .'.

Ingredients

100g/3½oz dark chocolate
4 eggs
150g/5½oz caster sugar
150g/5½oz ground almonds

Serves 10

Line the base and sides of a 20cm (8 inch) round baking tin with non-stick baking paper. Grate the dark chocolate and set aside. With an electric beater beat the egg yolks together with the sugar for a few minutes until almost white. In a separate bowl beat the egg whites into stiff peaks. Slowly fold the ground almonds into the egg yolk mixture, then gently fold in the egg whites and the grated chocolate. Bake in an oven preheated to 160°C (325°F) for 45 minutes to 1 hour. Allow the cake to cool before serving either by itself or with Rich Chocolate Ice-cream (page 101).

Tips and variations

Use half ground almonds and half ground hazelnuts, or add a few blanched and ground apricot kernels (bitter almonds) to the mixture.

RETRO CAKE

I tasted this cake in a wonderful Italian restaurant in Tokyo and, although I never got the actual recipe, I tried to reproduce it at home, with good results. I call it 'retro' because of the wonderful and unusual topping, which resembles a 1970s fabric.

Ingredients

5 eggs, separated
150g/5$\frac{1}{2}$oz sugar
grated zest of 1 lemon
150g/5$\frac{1}{2}$oz flour (plain or high-grade)
25g/1oz butter, melted
4–5 tablespoons milk

TOPPING
2 egg yolks
4 tablespoons sugar
100ml/3$\frac{1}{2}$fl oz white wine

50g/2oz dark chocolate

FILLING
1 egg
2 tablespoons sugar
1 tablespoon plain flour
300ml/10$\frac{1}{2}$fl oz milk
1–2 drops vanilla essence

50g/2oz dark chocolate

Serves 12

Partly fill a small saucepan with hot water and set over a medium heat. Set a bowl over the simmering water and whisk the egg yolks together with the sugar until they are light and foamy. Remove from the stove and add the lemon zest, then the flour, gradually, and finally the melted butter. Add the milk to thin the mixture. In a separate bowl beat the egg whites into stiff peaks, then fold into the mixture. Line the base of a 23cm (9 inch) round baking tin with non-stick baking paper, then grease and flour the sides of the tin. Pour the mixture into the tin and bake in an oven preheated to 180°C (350°F) for 25–30 minutes or until a toothpick inserted into the cake comes out clean. Allow the cake to cool in the tin for a few minutes.

To prepare the topping, partly fill a small saucepan with hot water and set over a medium heat. Set a small bowl over the simmering water and whisk the egg yolks together with the sugar, then add the wine. Keep whisking until thick and frothy. Remove from heat and allow it to cool to room temperature, stirring from time to time.

To prepare the filling, whisk the egg together with the sugar and flour in a small saucepan. Slowly add the milk and bring to the boil, stirring continuously. When the mixture thickens stir in the vanilla essence and remove from heat.

Cut the cake horizontally into 2 discs and, leaving a circular space in the middle, pour $\frac{2}{3}$ of the filling over the bottom disc. Chop the chocolate into small pieces and stir into the remaining custard – it should melt quickly on stirring, otherwise gently reheat it. Pour the chocolate custard into the centre of the bottom disc and cover the cake with the top disc.

To complete the cake, pour the topping over the cake, covering the top and sides evenly. Put the topping chocolate in a small plastic bag and seal, then place in a pot of hot water and allow it to melt. Cut a tiny hole at the base of the plastic bag and squeeze straight lines of chocolate across the cake, about 1cm ($\frac{1}{2}$ inch) apart. Run a toothpick at right angles across the lines, either in the same direction, or alternate directions, to create a wavy pattern. Refrigerate to allow the topping to set before cutting.

Tips and variations

Try making the topping with red wine. It tastes even better although the colour is not so appealing. For a more intense flavour, brush the 2 discs with liqueur before filling.

TORTA BAROZZI - CHOCOLATE AND COFFEE CAKE

This is an incredibly yummy chocolate brownie-like cake from Vignola, a small city near Modena, in Italy's Emilia-Romagna region. The original recipe is patented, but every household in the area makes it, with this being my own version. After tasting it, a friend (who prefers to remain anonymous) said it was 'better than sex'.

Ingredients

100g/3½oz dark chocolate
130g/4½oz butter
200g/7oz sugar
3 eggs, separated
30g/1oz arrowroot (or potato flour)
30g/1oz cocoa
2 teaspoons espresso coffee powder

Serves 8–10

Melt the chocolate and butter together until soft enough to work with a spoon. Remove from the heat and stir in the sugar, then the egg yolks, arrowroot, cocoa and coffee. In a separate bowl beat the egg whites into stiff peaks, then fold into the mixture. Pour into a 20cm (8 inch) baking tin lined with non-stick baking paper and bake in an oven preheated to 180°C (350°F) for 40 minutes. Allow to cool and cut the next day (or it will disintegrate).

Tips and variations

It is very important to use proper coffee for Italian mocha machines, not instant or filter coffee. The chocolate should be the best dark cooking chocolate you can find, with 70 percent cocoa solids. Potato flour is very common in Italy and it is used for a variety of cakes, but in this recipe it can be substituted with arrowroot. This cake can be baked in a square tin and cut into smaller squares, then dusted with icing sugar and cocoa on alternate pieces for a chessboard effect.

CIAMBELLA ALLA RICOTTA

The use of ricotta instead of butter gives this cake a unique texture which is light and fragrant.

Ingredients

250g/8½oz pot ricotta cheese
300g/10½oz sugar
3 eggs
300g/1½oz self-raising flour
grated rind of 1 lemon
1–2 teaspoons blueberry or plum jam
brown sugar to sprinkle

Serves 12

Cream together the ricotta and the sugar, then add the eggs, flour and lemon rind. Pour into a 20cm (8 inch) non-stick ring tin, greased with butter. Dot a few teaspoons of jam on top, not too close to the edges, and gently press the jam down into the cake mixture. Sprinkle with brown sugar. Bake in an oven preheated to 180°C (350°F) for approximately 40 minutes or until a toothpick inserted into the cake comes out clean. Allow the ciambella to cool in the tin for a few minutes, then turn it out and allow it to cool upside-down for a few more minutes before turning onto a serving plate. Eat only when completely cool, perhaps accompanied by a cappuccino.

Tips and variations

Dark and slightly tangy jams are suited to this recipe, but the choice is yours. Add a few sultanas to the mixture instead of the jam. Make this cake for Easter and place a large chocolate Easter egg in the centre. For an easy ricotta Savarin, follow the same recipe, omitting the jam. Leave the hot cake upside down and drench with syrup made from water, sugar and liqueur. Cool and serve with whipped cream and strawberries in the centre.

SACHER TORTE

The Sacher Torte is the most celebrated Viennese cake, created in the early 19th century by Franz Sacher, who worked at the court of Metternich — some claim as a pastry chef, while others say that at the time he was only a 16-year-old apprentice. To this day, the original recipe remains secret, still held by the renowned Hotel Sacher in Vienna. This one, of course, is my own homemade version. (See photo on page 24)

Ingredients

150g/5½oz unsalted butter
150g/5½oz sugar
150g/5½oz dark chocolate, melted
1 tablespoon cocoa
5 eggs, separated
50g/2oz ground almonds
100g/3½oz flour (plain or high-grade)

FILLING AND TOPPING
8 tablespoons apricot jam
5 tablespoons hot water
100g/3½oz dark chocolate

whipped cream to serve (optional)

Serves 10–12

Line the base of a 20cm (8 inch) round baking tin with non-stick baking paper, then grease and flour the sides of the tin. In a large mixing bowl cream the butter and sugar together, then add the melted chocolate, cocoa, and the egg yolks, one by one. In a separate bowl beat the egg whites with a pinch of salt into stiff peaks. Add the ground almonds to the chocolate mixture and alternately fold in 2 tablespoons of egg white and 1 tablespoon of flour, until all the ingredients are folded in together. This can take some time. Pour the mixture into the baking tin and bake in an oven preheated to 180°C (350°F) for approximately 45 minutes or until a toothpick inserted in the cake comes out clean. Allow the cake to cool, then cut it into 2 discs and fill with 5 tablespoons of the apricot jam. Thin the remaining 3 tablespoons of jam with 2 tablespoons of hot water and spread over the top of the cake. Melt the dark chocolate with the remaining hot water and spread over the cake top and sides. Serve by itself or with whipped cream.

Tips and variations

Some Sacher variations have jam only under the topping and not in the centre. Although not traditional, raspberry jam is also excellent.

AMARETTO FLAN WITH APRICOTS AND AMARETTO CARAMEL

One of my favourite creations, this flan tastes complex but is very easy to make.

Ingredients

100g/3½oz amaretti biscuits
100g /3½oz savoiardi or sponge biscuits
300ml/10½fl oz milk
2 eggs, separated
2 tablespoons brown (or Moscovado) sugar
10 apricots and whipped
   cream (optional) to serve

CARAMEL SAUCE
6 tablespoons water
3 tablespoons brown (or Moscovado) sugar
6 tablespoons Amaretto liqueur

Serves 10

■ Break all the biscuits into small pieces into a bowl, pour over the milk and leave to soak. In a separate bowl beat the egg yolks and sugar together until pale yellow and foamy. Add the biscuit and milk mixture. Beat the egg whites into stiff peaks, then fold into the mixture. Line a 23cm (9 inch) round tin with non-stick baking paper and pour in the mixture. Bake in an oven preheated to 160°C (325°F) for approximately 30 minutes or until the top is dark brown and a toothpick inserted in the centre of the cake comes out clean. Meanwhile prepare the sauce. In a heavy-based saucepan mix the water, sugar and Amaretto liqueur. Stir until it smells like caramel and starts to thicken (1–2 minutes). This caramel does not need to 'burn' or become sticky like the classic caramel. Pour half the caramel over the hot cake, without removing it from the tin, then allow the cake to cool. Before serving slice open the apricots and remove the stones, then place the apricots under the grill for 1–2 minutes until lightly browned. Pour the remaining caramel over the apricot halves and serve, 2 halves per slice of cake, accompanied by whipped cream, if desired.

Tips and variations

If you don't have amaretto biscuits, use macaroon biscuits and save 5 apricot stones, remove the kernels from inside, blanch them in boiling water to remove the skin, then crush them and add to the cake mixture. Make a double quantity of caramel and mix some with the whipped cream. For a citrus flavour, substitute the Amaretto liqueur with Grand Marnier or Cointreau.

TORTA BELLA

While experimenting in the kitchen I came up with this cake, which I truly love. Of course the better and richer the white chocolate, the better the results – so if you can afford it, go for Belgian chocolate.

Ingredients

300g/10½oz white chocolate
150g/5½oz unsalted butter
5 eggs, separated
100g/3½oz sugar
2 tablespoons plain flour
icing sugar for dusting

CHOCOLATE STRAWBERRIES
20 strawberries, with stems
200g/7oz white chocolate
edible gold paper to decorate (optional)

Serves 12

Melt the white chocolate together with the butter and set aside to cool. In a large mixing bowl whisk the egg yolks and sugar together until pale yellow and foamy (it is better to do this by hand). While still whisking, add the cooled chocolate mixture, then the flour. In a separate bowl beat the egg whites into stiff peaks and gently fold into the mixture. Line the base and sides of a 23cm (9 inch) round cake tin with non-stick baking paper. Pour in the mixture and bake in an oven preheated to 180°C (350°F) for approximately 35 minutes or until a toothpick inserted into the cake comes out clean. Remove the cake from the oven, dust with icing sugar, and allow it to cool in the tin for 2–3 hours. It will flatten while cooling, just like a soufflé. To prepare the chocolate strawberries, lightly rinse and dry the strawberries. Melt the chocolate and, holding each strawberry by the stem, dip it halfway into the chocolate. Place the strawberries, chocolate end up, on a cooling tray to set, attaching a small piece of edible gold paper, if desired. Lift the cake from its tin by the baking paper and remove the paper. Place the cake on a serving plate and arrange the strawberries on top.

Tips and variations

Dark chocolate can be used instead of white chocolate, with ¼ teaspoon of chilli powder added to the cake mixture. The result is a rich, intense cake with an unusual bite to it.

Pumpkin Crème Caramel - see recipe on page 65

Spoon Desserts

The definition of this chapter is self-explanatory – these desserts should be eaten with a spoon! The only slight exception here is the sweet ravioli, which is best served with a dessert fork. The ravioli are among the few hot desserts in this section, along with the individual apricot steam puddings and the chocolate soufflés. For the rest, cold dessert treats like panna cotta, blancmange and coffee crème are just a few ideas to inspire you to create more sophisticated and delicate crèmes and puddings. Choose desserts from this chapter for a special occasion or to end a formal dinner party. They are usually easier to make than they seem and they will always create a great impression.

BLANCMANGE WITH ICED PEACHES AND BLUEBERRIES

Blancmange is an almond jelly which, a few centuries ago, was very popular in France and Italy (where it is known as *bianco mangiare*). Delicate and white like panna cotta, this spoon dessert is very easy to make if you use good commercial almond milk, or you can make your own.

Ingredients

BLANCMANGE
500ml/17fl oz almond milk
2 tablespoons sugar
½ teaspoon agar agar powder
1 tablespoon plus 1 teaspoon
   Amaretto liqueur

PEACHES
4 ripe peaches
2 tablespoons lemon juice
2 tablespoons icing sugar

BLUEBERRIES
120g/4oz blueberries
1 teaspoon icing sugar
1–2 drops lemon or lime juice

Serves 4

To make the blancmange, put the almond milk, sugar, agar agar and 1 tablespoon of Amaretto liqueur into a saucepan, bring to the boil and simmer for 1–2 minutes. Test 1 teaspoonful of the liquid, which should thicken when cool if the agar agar is completely dissolved. Distribute the remaining teaspoon of Amaretto liqueur over 4 individual dessert moulds or cups and divide the hot mixture between them. Allow to cool before refrigerating. To prepare the peaches, blanch them in boiling water for 1 minute, then remove the skin. Roll them in the lemon juice, then in the icing sugar. Place them in a bowl, cover, leave for 1–2 hours at room temperature, then refrigerate. To prepare the blueberries, mix them in a bowl with the icing sugar and lemon or lime juice. Stir to completely coat the berries, then refrigerate. To serve the dessert, ease each blancmange onto an individual dessert plate using the handle of a teaspoon, and pour over the juice from the peaches. Finely slice the peaches and decorate the blancmanges with the blueberries and peaches.

Tips and variations

To make almond milk, blanch 250g (8½oz) of best quality almonds, plus 10 bitter almonds (apricot kernels) and remove the skins. Blend the almonds with 500ml (1 pint) of boiling water. Strain through a muslin cloth, squeezing out as much milk as you can. Add sugar to taste.

CHOCOLATE SOUFFLÉS

I like this particular recipe because it doesn't taste too 'eggy', which is one of the main problems I find with soufflés. Timing is everything here, so prepare the chocolate mixture ahead of time, and when your guests have almost finished their main dish, beat the egg whites vigorously, then finish making the soufflés and put them in the oven.

Ingredients

1 egg
3 tablespoons sugar
1 tablespoon cocoa
1 tablespoon cornflour
200ml/7fl oz milk
50g/2oz butter, melted
2 egg whites
pinch of salt
¼ teaspoon cream of tartar
1 tablespoon caster sugar

Serves 6

Grease 6 individual ramekins with butter. In a heavy-based saucepan mix the egg with the sugar, add the cocoa and cornflour then, gradually, the milk. Bring to the boil and simmer until the mixture thickens. Remove from the heat, then add the melted butter, brushing a little over the top to prevent a skin from forming. Allow to cool. The soufflés can be prepared in advance to this stage. In a separate bowl beat the egg whites into very stiff peaks with the salt and cream of tartar, and continue to beat, adding the caster sugar at the end. Beat for 1–2 minutes, then tap the beaters with the excess egg white over the chocolate mixture and fold in to soften. Add the rest of the egg white to the chocolate mixture and fold in very carefully. Divide between the greased ramekins and place immediately in an oven preheated to 180°C (350°F) for approximately 20 minutes. Serve immediately.

Tips and variations

Do not open the oven door to check whether the soufflés have risen. If your oven door does not have a window, you should be able to tell by the delicious smell when they are ready. Add ½ teaspoon ground coffee or add another tablespoon of liqueur to the chocolate mixture to intensify the flavour. Grand Marnier or Frangelico are excellent. Substitute cocoa with a few drops of vanilla essence or the seeds of 1 vanilla pod, or 1 tablespoon of fruit jam.

BUDINO ALLA VANIGLIA - VANILLA PUDDING

Budino is a very Italian dessert, usually vanilla- or chocolate-flavoured, but once you master this basic recipe, many more flavours and variations are possible. Usually I make budino as an impromptu dessert with the help of my children, and with whatever ingredients are to hand. For this recipe I add cream, which makes it velvety smooth. Budino is also suitable as a pastry or cake filling.

Ingredients

2 eggs
3 tablespoons sugar
1 tablespoon plain flour
300ml/10fl oz cream (single or double)
300ml/10fl oz milk
1 vanilla pod, or 2 drops vanilla essence

Serves 8

■ Break the eggs into a heavy-based saucepan, add the sugar and flour and stir, making sure there are no lumps. Add the cream and milk, then the vanilla pod (vanilla essence, if used, is added later) and gently bring the mixture to the boil. Continue stirring until the mixture thickens, taking care not to let it catch on the bottom of the saucepan. When cooked the budino should be creamy and not taste of flour. Remove from the heat and add the vanilla essence, if using. Divide the mixture between 8 small bowls and allow to cool at room temperature before refrigerating for 2–3 hours. Budino is perfect by itself, but for a special occasion decorate with berries, thin slices of kiwifruit, whipped cream or chocolate shavings.

Tips and variations

For a chocolate version, break 100g (3½oz) dark chocolate into small pieces and stir into the cooked mixture until melted. For a lemon flavour, add the zest of 1 lemon, and for coffee-flavoured budino add 50ml (2fl oz) espresso coffee. Budino is also excellent flavoured with any liqueur or fruit purée.

CHOCOLATE AND RUM MOUSSE

This mousse tastes very rich and complex, but the recipe is extremely easy and uses only a few ingredients. It does not require gelatine, making it suitable for vegetarians, and it can be prepared a day in advance.

Ingredients

3 eggs, separated
3 teaspoons brown (or Moscovado) sugar
15ml/½fl oz dark rum
100g/3½oz dark chocolate, melted
250ml/8½fl oz whipping cream
whipped cream to serve (optional)
chocolate shavings (optional)

Serves 6

Half fill a medium saucepan with warm water and set over a medium heat. In a bowl whisk the egg yolks together with the sugar using a balloon whisk or electric beater, then add the rum. Set the bowl over the saucepan of simmering water and continue to whisk the egg mixture until creamy and frothy. Remove the bowl from the heat. Melt the chocolate and slowly add to the egg mixture, folding it in with a spatula. Allow to cool, stirring from time to time. In a separate bowl beat the egg whites into stiff peaks. In another bowl whip the cream. When the cream is almost stiff, add the egg whites and whip for a further 30 seconds. Slowly add the chocolate mixture, whipping slowly and continuously. Pour into 6 serving bowls and refrigerate for at least 2 hours before serving. Decorate with whipped cream and/or dark chocolate shavings, if desired.

Tips and variations

When melting chocolate, use a miniature whisk or a chopstick, which stirs well and has very little surface for the chocolate to stick to and therefore get wasted. The best variations of this mousse are provided by the huge variety of liqueurs you can choose from. Cointreau gives a delicious chocolate and orange flavour. Coffee and berry liqueurs are also good. White and milk chocolate can also be used, however the flavour is less intense.

ROSEMARY AND LEMON SYLLABUB

This must be the easiest dessert ever – the taste is distinctive, a bit like zabaglione, but it takes only a fraction of the time to prepare. Serve the syllabub the same day you make it, as it is not meant to keep.

Ingredients

150ml/5fl oz sweet sherry
3 tablespoons caster sugar
1 tablespoon lemon juice
sprig of rosemary
300ml/10fl oz whipping cream
lemon rind, rosemary sprigs and
    flowers to decorate

Serves 6

Place the sherry, sugar, lemon juice and sprig of rosemary in a bowl and allow to infuse for 1 hour or more. Discard the rosemary and add the cream, whipping until stiff. Divide the mixture between six serving glasses and decorate with lemon rind, small rosemary sprigs and flowers.

Tips and variations

Substitute sherry with sweet white wine, or the rosemary with lavender or sage (including the flowers, which are all the same colour).

COCONUT AND WHITE CHOCOLATE DREAM

Coconut and chocolate go together incredibly well, and canned coconut milk is so easy to use for this quick and luscious dessert.

Ingredients

2 egg yolks
3 tablespoons sugar
1 tablespoon cornflour
400ml/13fl oz (1 can) coconut milk or cream
100g/3½oz white chocolate, chopped
strawberries and desiccated coconut
    to decorate (optional)

Serves 4–6

In a heavy-based saucepan beat the egg yolks with the sugar until pale yellow and foamy. Add the cornflour and stir, then add the coconut milk. Place the saucepan over a medium heat and, stirring continuously, add the white chocolate. Bring slowly to the boil and simmer for 1–2 minutes, before pouring into 4–6 cups or small bowls. Refrigerate before serving and decorate with a strawberry tossed in desiccated coconut, if desired.

Tips and variations

Use very tiny bowls, cups or glasses to make miniature desserts and top with strawberries. They will look very effective on a dessert selection plate. Milk or dark chocolate can be used for a more chocolatey taste.

DULCE DE LECHE PUDDING

This dessert is sweet and intense – a crunchy dark chocolate topping, followed by a creamy caramel, then the strong taste of brandy. Dulce de leche (a sweetened milk) is a speciality of Argentina, and it may be difficult to source outside South America. I use canned caramelised cream instead, but you can make your own caramel with condensed milk. If you can source the Argentinian dulce de leche, it makes this dessert truly special.

Ingredients

1 x 380g/13oz can caramelised cream or
   dulce de leche
250ml/8½fl oz milk
3 egg yolks
100g/3½oz stale sponge, brioche or
   panettone
6 teaspoons brandy
50g/2oz dark chocolate

Serves 6

■ Mix the caramelised cream (or dulce de leche) and milk in a saucepan, stirring until there are no lumps. Add the egg yolks and simmer, stirring continuously, for 1–2 minutes until the mixture thickens. Remove from the heat. Crumble the stale cake and divide between 6 individual serving bowls, moistening each one with 1 teaspoon of liqueur. Use slightly more liqueur if the cake is hard. Cover with the caramel mixture and allow the desserts to cool to room temperature, then refrigerate for 1–2 hours until the caramel is set. Melt the chocolate and pour a small quantity over each dessert, spreading it to the edges. Refrigerate again before serving.

Tips and variations

To make your own caramel reduce 2 x 380g (13oz) cans of sweetened condensed milk to half the quantity over a low heat until caramel-coloured. Rum, whisky or cognac can be used instead of brandy, but do not substitute with a sweet liqueur. If you find the Dulce de Leche too sweet but like the idea of a brandy base and a crunchy chocolate topping, try the recipes for Budino alla Vaniglia (page 53) or perhaps Vanilla Panna Cotta (page 64).

CRÈME BRÛLÉE WITH NECTARINES

This is my own version of crème brûlée, the classic French dessert which literally means 'burnt cream', and is one of my favourite desserts. It is important that the sugary top is crunchy, the crème velvety and rich, and the fruit at the bottom refreshing. The dessert is complete in itself – just serve with a spoon.

Ingredients

3 egg yolks
3 tablespoons caster sugar
300ml/10fl oz cream (single or double)
2 drops vanilla essence
2 nectarines
4 teaspoons brown (or Moscovado) sugar

Serves 4

Half fill a medium saucepan with warm water and set over a medium heat. Whisk the egg yolks and sugar together in a bowl until pale yellow and foamy. Continue beating and slowly add the cream, then the vanilla essence. Set the bowl over the saucepan of simmering water and continue to whisk until the cream thickens (about 10 minutes). Wash and finely slice the nectarines, then divide between 4 ramekins and cover with the crème. Refrigerate for at least 6 hours. One hour before serving put 1 teaspoon of brown sugar on each dessert, spreading it evenly to the edges. Place under a preheated hot grill for 1–2 minutes. Do not close the grill door and watch the desserts carefully, as they can easily burn. When the sugar changes colour and becomes shiny, remove the dishes from under the grill, cool at room temperature, then return them to the refrigerator. Serve within 1 hour to ensure the top remains crunchy.

Tips and variations

The longer you leave this dessert after grilling, the softer the sugar will become. Fresh blueberries can be used instead of nectarines, but most other fruit tends to become too watery under the weight of the crème.

FRUIT OF THE FOREST TIRAMISÙ

I created this summery tiramisù for my children, who are too young to enjoy my coffee and whisky version, and for everyone who wants to make the most of the berry season.

Ingredients

500g/1lb 2oz mixed berries (strawberries, raspberries, blueberries, blackberries or boysenberries)
1 teaspoon lemon juice
2 tablespoons sugar
1 egg, separated
200ml/7fl oz whipping cream
250g/9oz mascarpone
1 x 250g/9oz packet savoiardi or sponge biscuits (approximately 20 biscuits)
mint leaves to serve (optional)

Serves 10–12

Lightly rinse and dry the strawberries, cut into small slices, setting a few whole strawberries aside for decoration, if desired. Put the strawberry slices in a large bowl with the other berries, add the lemon juice and half of the sugar, and allow the berries to marinate for 1–2 hours. Beat the egg white into stiff peaks. In a separate bowl lightly whip the cream. In another bowl beat the egg yolk with the remaining sugar until pale yellow. Fold the fruit, egg white, cream and egg yolk mixture into the mascarpone and set aside. Cover the base of a 5cm (2 inch) deep 20 x 20cm (8 x 8 inch) serving dish with half the biscuits. Pour over half the berries and their juice as evenly as possible to soak all the biscuits. Cover the biscuits with half of the mascarpone cream, then repeat with the remaining ingredients. Refrigerate for at least 6 hours, preferably overnight, and serve, decorated with the whole strawberries, a few berries and mint leaves, if desired.

Tips and variations

Instead of berries use seasonal fruit such as peaches and nectarines, mango and papaya, or pineapple and bananas. Add a dash of whisky or your favourite liqueur to the marinating fruit for a more intense flavour if serving to adults. Use sponge cake instead of biscuits. Two stacked sponges will make a tall and impressive dessert.

ÎLES FLOTTANTES - FLOATING ISLANDS

A traditional French recipe given to me by Hélène, the delightful mother of a friend from Aix-en-Provence. This dessert is better if prepared on the day it is served, and is an ideal complement to a formal dinner.

Ingredients

500ml/17fl oz milk
75g/2½oz sugar
1 vanilla pod
3 eggs, separated
pinch of salt

CARAMEL
20 sugar cubes
water

Serves 4–6

In a broad-based saucepan bring the milk to a gentle simmer with half of the sugar and the vanilla pod. Do not allow the milk to boil over. In a bowl beat the egg whites with a pinch of salt into stiff peaks. Using two tablespoons, shape the egg whites into egg-sized 'islands' and poach them lightly in the hot milk two at a time, for no more than 1 minute, then gently lift the 'islands' onto a plate (makes about 12 'islands'). Keep the milk warm. Beat the egg yolks together with the remaining sugar until light and pale yellow. Remove the vanilla pod from the milk, then add the egg yolk mixture and bring to the boil, stirring continuously until a thin custard forms. Pour the custard into a large serving bowl with a flat base and arrange the white islands on top. Prepare the caramel by spraying the sugar cubes with water, then melting them in a heavy-based or non-stick pan until brown. Pour the hot caramel over the dessert and refrigerate until ready to serve.

Tips and variations

If the eggs curdle when making the custard, beat vigorously, preferably with an immersion food processor, until the consistency is creamy again. For a sweeter, 'eggier' custard use 4 eggs and 100g/3½oz of sugar, which is closer to the original recipe. If you are not keen on caramel, top the dessert with slivered almonds or grated chocolate before serving. Another topping variation with thin strips of lemon zest is known as *dame-blanche*.

APRICOT STEAM PUDDINGS

Fluffy and light, these little individual puddings are the perfect ending to a warm traditional winter meal.

Ingredients

4–6 teaspoons apricot jam
50g/2oz savoiardi or sponge biscuits
4 dried apricots
150ml/5fl oz milk
2 eggs, separated
3 tablespoons sugar
50g/2oz ground almonds
cream, crème anglaise or chocolate
   sauce to serve

Serves 4–6

Grease 6 small or 4 medium individual pudding bowls with butter, and dust with flour. Place a small piece of non-stick baking paper on the bottom of each pudding bowl and add 1 teaspoon of apricot jam. Break the biscuits into a bowl. Chop the dried apricots into small pieces, add to the biscuits and cover with the milk. Beat the egg yolks with the sugar until pale yellow and frothy. Add the biscuit mixture and ground almonds. In another bowl, beat the egg whites into stiff peaks and gently fold into the mixture. Fill the pudding bowls with the mixture, cover with non-stick baking paper or tin foil and secure with a string or elastic band. Gently steam the puddings for 40–45 minutes. These puddings are delicious hot but may also be served cold. Serve with a jug of pouring cream, crème anglaise or chocolate sauce.

Tips and variations

Use grated chocolate instead of apricot jam for a great-tasting pudding. A few berries or cherries, fresh or frozen, add colour for a special occasion. Either place them at the bottom of the ramekins or add them to the pudding mixture.

COFFEE CRÈME

A truly decadent dessert, this is best served in espresso coffee cups, as a little goes a long way!

Ingredients

2 egg yolks
3 tablespoons sugar
100ml/3½fl oz espresso coffee
200ml/7fl oz whipping cream
25g/1oz milk chocolate
4–6 cherries

Serves 4–6

Half fill a medium saucepan with warm water and set over a medium heat. Whisk the egg yolks and sugar together in a small bowl until pale yellow and foamy, then slowly add the coffee and half of the cream. Set the bowl over the saucepan of simmering water and continue to whisk the mixture until it thickens (about 10 minutes). Chop the chocolate into small pieces and mix in until it melts. Divide between 4–6 espresso coffee cups or small serving bowls. Allow to cool to room temperature, then refrigerate for 1–2 hours. Before serving, whip the remaining cream. Top each dessert with whipped cream and decorate with a fresh cherry.

Tips and variations

Top with chocolate curls if cherries are unavailable. Add a pinch of cinnamon to the mixture and decorate with a cinnamon stick. Substitute the coffee with cooled cocoa and the milk chocolate with white chocolate.

LEMON CRÈME

This is a variation of my father's simple lemon crème, a light dessert suitable for all the family. My father places half a lemon (including the peel) in the crème and cools it in a large serving bowl. My mother enjoys this way of serving the crème, but it is quite impractical unless you like to lick the lemon, as she does.

Ingredients

1 egg
2 tablespoons sugar
1 tablespoon non-glutinous rice flour
500ml/17fl oz milk
zest of 1 lemon
1 teaspoon lemon juice

Serves 4

In a heavy-based saucepan mix the egg, sugar and rice flour together. Add the milk and lemon zest and gently bring to the boil. Continue stirring until the mixture thickens. Remove from the heat and add the lemon juice. Pour into 4 individual serving bowls, cool at room temperature, then refrigerate until set.

Tips and variations

It is very important to use a non-glutinous rice flour for this recipe. The crème can be used for a lemon crème brûlée (page 58).

VANILLA PANNA COTTA

A very fashionable Italian dessert, panna cotta now appears on the menu in many good cafés and restaurants around the world. This dessert is extremely easy to make, and its subtle taste makes it suitable for many variations.

Ingredients

500ml/17fl oz cream (double)
500ml/17fl oz milk
4 tablespoons sugar
$2/3$ teaspoon agar agar powder
1 vanilla pod
4 teaspoons Frangelico, Amaretto or other
   liqueur (optional)

Serves 8

Put the cream, milk, sugar, agar agar and the vanilla pod in a saucepan, bring to the boil and simmer for 1–2 minutes. Test 1 teaspoonful of the liquid, which should thicken when cool if the agar agar is completely dissolved. Splash 8 individual dessert moulds with ½ teaspoon each of the liqueur and divide the hot mixture between them. Allow to cool completely, then refrigerate. To assemble, ease each dessert onto a small dessert plate with the handle of a teaspoon and serve, either by itself or accompanied by fruit, such as strawberries and mango, and a thin biscuit.

Tips and variations

Instead of liqueur use cherry syrup, which will give a pink hue. Food colouring can be used for different colours. If you prefer a more delicate taste, use only ½ teaspoon of agar agar, and serve the panna cotta in their individual dishes. Panna cotta can be flavoured with anything – chocolate, coffee, caramel sauce, fruit sauces (blueberries are particularly good), and it can be brûléed (page 58). Make miniature panna cotta of different flavours for a mixed dessert assortment.

PUMPKIN CRÈME CARAMEL

Hands up all pumpkin lovers! This sophisticated little dessert is visually stunning – beautiful bright orange with a perfect caramel sauce on top. *(See photo on page 48)*

Ingredients

500g/1lb 2oz pumpkin, cleaned and peeled
300ml/10fl oz milk
6 tablespoons sugar
1 vanilla pod
3 egg yolks

CARAMEL
100g/3½oz sugar cubes
6 tablespoons water

Serves 8

■ Cut the pumpkin into small pieces and place in a saucepan with the milk, half the sugar and the vanilla pod, split open. Cook gently until the pumpkin is soft, taking care not to let the milk boil over. Meanwhile prepare the caramel. Place the sugar cubes and the water in a heavy-based saucepan and continue stirring until it forms a soft brown caramel (2–3 minutes). Divide the caramel into 8 individual moulds, lightly greased with butter. Remove the vanilla pod from the pumpkin mixture, pour into a blender or food processor and liquidise. In a separate bowl beat the egg yolks together with the remaining sugar until pale yellow and foamy. Add the warm pumpkin mixture and stir well. Divide between the 8 ramekins and bake in an oven preheated to 100°C (230°F) for 1 hour. Allow to cool, then refrigerate overnight. Before serving, ease each dessert onto a small serving plate with the handle of a teaspoon, and serve with a spoon.

Tips and variations

With traditional crème caramel, the ramekins are usually placed in a baking dish half filled with water while cooking, but this should not be necessary with the pumpkin version, as long as the oven temperature is low. For other vegetable variations use 300g (10½ oz) of carrots or kumara (sweet potato) instead of pumpkin.

MONTE BIANCO

There are hundreds of variations of this fabulous dessert, inspired by the famous mountain, but because it may be difficult to source fresh or dried chestnuts, I propose two recipes, one with chestnut purée, and one with fresh chestnuts, which takes longer but is more traditional. French or Italian chestnut purée is available in most delicatessen stores.

Ingredients

CHESTNUT PURÉE VERSION
500ml/1 pint whipping cream
1 x 500g/1lb 2oz can sweetened
    chestnut purée
1 x 439g/15$\frac{1}{2}$oz can unsweetened
    chestnut purée
100g/3$\frac{1}{2}$oz dark chocolate, finely grated

FRESH CHESTNUT VERSION
1kg/2lb 3oz fresh chestnuts
1 bay leaf (optional)
500ml/17fl oz whipping cream
200g/7oz dark chocolate, finely grated
1 drop vanilla essence or rum (optional)
chocolate curls (optional)
marrons glacés (optional)

Serves 12

To make the chestnut purée version, whip the cream until stiff. Fold the sweetened and unsweetened purées together with ¾ of the grated chocolate and ¾ of the whipped cream. Carefully spoon the mixture onto a serving plate, creating a cone or 'mountain' shape. Smooth the sides of the cone with a spatula and cover with the remaining whipped cream and chocolate. Refrigerate for 4 hours, preferably overnight. Cut into small slices, as it is very filling, and serve with a spoon or dessert fork.

To make the fresh chestnut version, boil the chestnuts with the bay leaf, if using, in plenty of water for approximately 3 hours. To check whether the chestnuts are cooked, cut one open. The inside should be soft and mushy when ready. Once the chestnuts are ready, cut them open and scoop out the pulp, mashing it in a bowl with a food mouli or potato masher. Whip the cream until stiff. Add the grated chocolate, vanilla essence or rum, if using, and ⅔ of the whipped cream. Fold the 2 mixtures together. Carefully spoon the mixture onto a serving plate, creating a cone or 'mountain' shape. Smooth the sides of the cone with a spatula and cover with the remaining whipped cream and chocolate. Refrigerate for 4 hours, preferably overnight. Decorate with chocolate curls and marron glacés, if desired. Cut into small slices, as it is very filling, and serve with a spoon or dessert fork.

Tips and variations

When boiling fresh chestnuts, a pinch of salt may be used instead of the bay leaf. Dried chestnuts can be used instead of fresh chestnuts, but they still need to be boiled for a long time and mashed once the skins are removed. Serve marrons glacés only with the fresh chestnut version, as it is not as sweet as the chestnut purée version. The Monte Bianco paste can also be used to fill sponges heavily soaked in liqueur.

ZABAGLIONE

It's the beating that counts here with zabaglione. Calculate 1 egg yolk per person and adjust the quantities. You can use a half egg shell to measure the liqueur, which will give you a good 'egg to liqueur' ratio. The quantity does not need to be precise.

Ingredients

1 egg yolk
1 tablespoon sugar
1/2 egg shell Marsala wine

Serves 1

Half fill a medium saucepan with warm water and set over a medium heat. Whisk the egg yolk and sugar together in a bowl, then add the Marsala. Set the bowl over the saucepan of simmering water and continue beating until the mixture thickens and becomes frothy (about 10 minutes if whisking by hand). Serve cold or warm in champagne or shot glasses, accompanied by thin biscuits.

Tips and variations

If Marsala wine is not available use port or a sweet white wine. Zabaglione has many uses – as a topping for ice-cream; as a dip for fresh strawberries; in tiramisù instead of the simple egg yolk and sugar mixture (see below); in a trifle; or as a filling for choux and éclair pastries. Also try my Retro Cake (page 40).

TIRAMISÙ DI ALESSANDRA

This dessert was named, and consequently propagated, by my circle of Italian girlfriends. Now they all follow my recipe, which is quite different from the traditional one, as it is lighter and contains more alcohol.

Ingredients

3 eggs, separated
300ml/10fl oz whipping cream
1 tablespoon, plus 1 teaspoon sugar
15ml/1/2fl oz espresso coffee
15ml/1/2fl oz whisky
20 (one 250g/9oz packet) savoiardi or
    sponge biscuits
espresso coffee powder for dusting

Serves 10–12

Beat the egg whites into stiff peaks. Lightly whip the cream, then fold in the egg whites and beat together for a few seconds. In a separate bowl beat the egg yolks together with 1 tablespoon of sugar until runny. Add to the cream and egg white mixture and beat again for a few seconds. In a wide soup bowl mix the espresso coffee, whisky and the remaining sugar and quickly dip the savoiardi biscuits, sugary side only, in the liquid. Arrange the biscuits, soaked side up, in a 5cm (2 inch) deep 20 x 20cm / 8 x 8 inch serving dish. Spoon over a little more coffee liquid if the biscuits look dry. Spread half of the cream mixture over the biscuits and repeat with the remaining ingredients. Bang the dish on the working surface to remove any air bubbles in the dessert, and refrigerate for 4 hours, preferably overnight. One hour before serving dust with plenty of ground Italian espresso coffee. Refrigerate again. Cut into squares and serve.

Tips and variations

Brandy can be used instead of whisky. For a more traditional version, sprinkle the top with cocoa instead of coffee.

SWEET RAVIOLI WITH LEMON BUTTER AND POPPY SEEDS

Sweet filled pasta is becoming quite a popular dessert in trendy cafés and restaurants. This recipe can be very versatile, with a great range of possible fillings and condiments.

Ingredients

FILLING
2 apples
20g/¾oz unsalted butter
1 tablespoon sugar
1–2 drops lemon juice
10–12 amaretti biscuits, crushed

PASTA
100g/3½oz flour (plain or high-grade)
1 egg

LEMON BUTTER
50g/2oz unsalted butter
2 tablespoons caster sugar
1 tablespoon lemon juice
poppy seeds to sprinkle

Serves 4

To make the filling, peel and cut the apples into small pieces, put in a saucepan, add the butter, sugar and lemon juice, and sauté on a low heat. When the apples start to disintegrate add the crushed amaretti biscuits. Remove from the heat and cover. To make the pasta, mix the flour and egg together. Knead to a smooth soft dough and then pass through the rollers of a pasta machine to make 4 sheets of very thin pasta of equal length. Spoon the filling over 2 of the sheets to make 16 ravioli portions. Cover with the second 2 sheets, cut into squares and press the edges together to seal. To make the lemon butter, cream the butter together with the caster sugar and lemon juice. In a large saucepan cook the pasta in plenty of water with a pinch of salt. To test if the ravioli are done, remove one from the water with a slotted spoon and pinch the corner. It should be soft and not too al dente. Scoop the ravioli out one by one and arrange on 4 dessert plates. Put a small amount of the lemon butter on top of each serving and sprinkle with poppy seeds. Serve immediately, accompanied by the remaining lemon butter.

Tips and variations

Substitute apples with pears, peaches or plums, and amaretti with other kinds of biscuits. Use brandy instead of lemon for the butter sauce, or drizzle with honey or maple syrup instead of the sweet lemon sauce.

ZUPPA INGLESE - ITALIAN TRIFLE

This is a classic Italian dessert, and a favourite in many households and restaurants across the country. The best part is the alcohol in the sponge, which can be adjusted to taste.

Ingredients

2 eggs
4 tablespoons sugar
2 tablespoons plain flour
1 litre/34fl oz, plus 200ml/7fl oz milk,
    for thinning the custard
50g/2oz unsalted butter
2 drops vanilla essence
100g/3½oz dark chocolate
100ml/3½fl oz red liqueur or mixture of
    cherry syrup and brandy
200g/7oz trifle sponge
200ml/7fl oz whipping cream
cherries, berries or grapes to decorate

Serves 10

Break the eggs into a heavy-based saucepan, add the sugar and flour and stir, ensuring there are no lumps. Add 1 litre (34fl oz) milk and the butter and bring to the boil. Continue stirring until the custard is creamy. Remove from the heat, add the vanilla essence and divide the custard equally into 2 bowls. Break the chocolate into small pieces and stir into one of the bowls of custard until melted. Pour the liqueur into a wide shallow dish, place the sponge in the dish to soak up all the liqueur.

To assemble, cut the soaked sponge horizontally in two and place one half in a glass bowl. Thin both custards with 100ml (3½fl oz) of milk. Layer the sponge with half the plain custard, followed by half the chocolate custard, allowing each custard layer to set before continuing. Repeat with the remaining ingredients. To serve, whip the cream, spread over the top and decorate with fruit.

Tips and variations

Make the custard with custard powder to shorten the preparation time. It also sets more quickly. Cherry syrup is available in delicatessen shops. As an alternative, use the liquid from a jar of preserved cherries. Use cognac or whisky instead of brandy, or a mixture of all three. To vary the texture, top with chopped hazelnuts and pistachio nuts, or small amaretti biscuits. Individual desserts, served in tall glasses, also look stunning.

Dairy-free Berry Muffins and Chocolate and Hazelnut Muffins - see recipes on pages 75 & 80

Biscuits & Small Treats

When there are many hungry mouths to feed, there is nothing better than a tin of biscuits, a basket of muffins, or an elegant tray of sweet delights. This chapter is ideal for those who like small things and love to work with their hands, creating shapes and wrapping delightful mini-surprises. The biscuit-maker, like the chocolatier, is the craftperson of patisserie. And because creativity is at its peak when we are small, I dedicate this chapter to all children, in body and mind.

BISCOTTI DI PRATO

Prato is a lovely city not far from Florence, a famous textile centre that is home to these biscotti. Also known as *cantucci*, these biscuits appear in variations all over the world.

Ingredients

150g/5oz sugar
2 eggs
250g/9oz flour (plain or strong)
1 teaspoon baking power
100g/3½oz unblanched almonds
1 teaspoon lemon or orange essence or
   Limoncino liqueur (optional)

Makes approximately 40 biscuits

Beat the sugar and eggs together, then add the remaining ingredients. Work the mixture with a wooden spoon. When the mixture thickens, use your hands to make one or two long rolls, about 7.5cm wide x 3cm high (3 x 1¼ inches) and bake in an oven preheated to 180°C (350°F) for 20–30 minutes. Turn the oven off, then cut the roll or rolls into small biscuits with a bread knife and return them to the warm oven for a further 10 minutes. Store in an airtight container.

Tips and variations

These biscuits are traditionally dipped into Vin Santo, a liqueur-type white wine, to soften them. If you prefer a paler crispier version of this biscuit, add 1–2 egg whites to the ingredients.

ALMOND AND CITRUS SWEETS

A truly indulgent and special treat, especially if you like almond- and marzipan-style sweets.

Ingredients

300g/10½oz sugar
100g/3½oz butter
3 eggs, separated
200g/7oz ground almonds
1 tablespoon arrowroot (or potato flour)
2 tablespoons citrus peel
1 tablespoon Amaretto liqueur (optional)

Makes approximately 25 sweets

Beat the sugar together with the butter, then mix in the egg yolks. Add the ground almonds, arrowroot, citrus peel and liqueur. In a separate bowl beat the egg whites into stiff peaks and fold into the almond mixture. Line a baking tray with non-stick baking paper, then spoon the almond mixture, 1 tablespoon at a time, onto the tray, leaving even spaces between the sweets. Bake in an oven preheated to 160°C (325°F) for 20–30 minutes. The sweets should turn golden on top and underneath when ready. Turn the oven off and allow the sweets to dry inside the oven, preferably overnight, until completely cold. Serve with coffee or a glass of sweet wine.

Tips and variations

To make these treats even more sweet and indulgent, cover them with melted dark chocolate. They keep well in a biscuit tin.

DAIRY-FREE BERRY MUFFINS

These muffins are extremely easy to make and taste delicious – without even a hint of milk or butter.
(See photo on page 72)

Ingredients

300g/10½oz self-raising flour
100g/3½oz sugar
100ml/3½fl oz vegetable oil
3 eggs
200ml/7fl oz water
1 teaspoon vanilla essence
pinch of salt
5 tablespoons frozen mixed berries
icing and berries to decorate (optional)

Makes 12 muffins

■ Place all the ingredients, except the berries, in a bowl and mix with an electric beater. When the mixture is smooth, fold in the frozen berries with a wooden spoon or spatula. Grease a 12-pan muffin tin or fill with paper cups and fill with the mixture. Bake in an oven preheated to 180°C (350°F) for approximately 25–30 minutes, or until the muffins are well risen and golden in colour. Decorate with icing and berries, if desired.

Tips and variations

This recipe can be used as a base for many variations of muffins. Add 1 tablespoon of cocoa, chopped nuts or sultanas to the mixture, or spoon a little jam into the centre of each muffin before baking. They are foolproof!

FRAPPE

In Italy, during the Carnival weeks in February, these traditional fried pastries can be seen piled high in trays in the shop windows of all the bakeries and patisseries. They are known by different names, depending on the city of origin, but are all similar in taste. Every city in Italy seems to have developed a distinctive shape, so you can be creative.

Ingredients

100g/3½oz self-raising flour
1 teaspoon icing sugar
1 tablespoon grappa
1 egg
flour for the board
plenty of oil for frying
plenty of icing sugar for dusting

Makes approximately 15 pieces

■ Mix the flour, icing sugar, grappa and egg in a bowl and work into a dough. Place it on a well-floured surface and roll out into a sheet about 3mm (⅛ inch) thick. A pasta machine can also be used at this stage. Cut the pastry into your preferred shapes – long strips that then can be knotted or looped, rectangular shapes that can be twisted into a bow, or passed through an incision made in the centre. Fry the pieces in plenty of hot oil, turning them when they become golden. Drain on absorbent paper and dust generously with icing sugar. Serve cold on a tray or large serving plate.

Tips and variations

The quantities can easily be doubled or tripled. Grappa can be substituted with brandy or lemon zest, but neither give the right taste! A similar but richer sweet is made by using the same pastry, then joining two pieces together with a mixture of chestnut purée, plum jam and chopped walnuts, or fruit mince. Fry as above, or bake until golden brown.

AMARETTI BISCUITS

There are so many ways of making amaretti biscuits that I have provided two recipes. The first is for soft amaretti, made with fresh almonds, and the second, a time-saver, uses ground almonds and makes crispier biscuits.

Ingredients

AMARETTI WITH FRESH ALMONDS

200g/7oz almonds
20 bitter almonds (apricot kernels)
3 egg whites
200g/7oz sugar
1 teaspoon arrowroot
grated zest of 1 lemon
brown sugar for sprinkling

Makes 30–35 biscuits

AMARETTI WITH GROUND ALMONDS

15 bitter almonds (apricot kernels)
1 teaspoon brown sugar
3 egg whites
3 tablespoons caster sugar
150g/5oz ground almonds
brown sugar for sprinkling

Makes 25 biscuits

To make Amaretti with fresh almonds, blanch the almonds and bitter almonds in boiling water for a few seconds, then remove the skins. Finely grind in a food processor. Beat the egg whites, sugar and arrowroot into very stiff peaks, then fold in the ground almonds and lemon zest. Spoon onto a baking tray lined with non-stick baking paper to make approximately 30 biscuits. Sprinkle with brown sugar and bake in an oven preheated to 100°C (225°F) for 45 minutes to 1 hour, or until they easily detach from the paper but before they become brown. Allow them to cool in the oven.

To make Amaretti with ground almonds, blanch the bitter almonds in boiling water for a few seconds, then remove the skins. Finely grind in a food processor with the brown sugar. Beat the egg whites and caster sugar together, then fold in the ground almonds and bitter almonds. Spoon onto a baking tray lined with non-stick baking paper to make approximately 25 biscuits. Sprinkle with brown sugar and bake in an oven preheated to 100°C (225°F) for 45 minutes to 1 hour, or until they easily detach from the paper but before they become brown. Allow them to cool in the oven. If the amaretti are too soft or chewy once cooked, reheat the oven to 180°C (350°F), turn it off, and place the amaretti back in to harden.

Tips and variations

Amaretti can be made crunchier by increasing the quantity of sugar and decreasing the amount of almonds. Wrap them in crêpe paper and offer as a gift in little boxes or in a jar with other biscuits. Commercial amaretti, which are widely available, are quite different. They are often used as ingredients in desserts and cakes.

PRETEND PEACHES

These sweet treats, which resemble peaches in colour and shape (hence their name), can be found in patisseries and cafes in the north of Italy and across the border in the Balkan countries. The original recipes are quite laborious and suitable only for making large quantities. Here is a quick version that can easily be made at home.

Ingredients

50g/2oz butter
100g/3½oz sugar
2 eggs
250g/9oz self-raising flour
50g/2oz dark chocolate

COATING
100ml/3½fl oz red liqueur or red fruit syrup
100g/3½oz sugar

Makes 12 'peaches'

Cream the butter and sugar together, add the eggs, then the flour and work into a soft dough. Line a baking tray with non-stick baking paper. With your hands shape the dough into 24 balls, each as big as a large walnut. Place the balls onto the baking tray and gently press them down to flatten the base, but keep the tops round. Bake in an oven preheated to 180°C (350°F) for 10 minutes. Melt the chocolate, then use it to sandwich the 'peach' halves together in pairs to make 12 'peaches'. When the chocolate is set roll them in a bowl filled with the red liqueur or syrup, then roll in a bowl of sugar. Allow the coating to dry. Serve with coffee or tea.

Tips and variations

Arrange your 'peaches' with equivalent-sized real peaches on a tray lined with fresh green leaves; the combination looks amazing! If red liqueur is not available, add a few drops of red food colouring to Amaretto or other sweet liqueur. Make smaller 'peaches' for a party tray – their colour will attract attention! Traditional fillings include crème anglaise or chocolate custard, but melted chocolate is certainly easier.

CHOCOLATE AND HAZELNUT MUFFINS

Chocolate and hazelnuts are a match made in heaven. In this recipe light cocoa muffins are filled with a milk chocolate and hazelnut paste. *(See photo on page 72)*

Ingredients

HAZELNUT PASTE
2 tablespoons hazelnuts, plus 12 whole
  nuts roasted
100g/3½oz milk chocolate
15g/½oz butter

MUFFINS
50g/2oz butter
200g/7oz sugar
2 eggs
1 tablespoon cocoa
150ml/5fl oz milk
250g/9oz self-raising flour

Makes 12 muffins

First prepare the hazelnut paste. In a food processor grind the 2 tablespoons of hazelnuts to a sticky paste. Melt the milk chocolate with the butter, then stir in the nut paste, working with a spoon until the ingredients are evenly mixed. To make the muffins, cream the butter, sugar and eggs together in a bowl with an electric beater. Add the cocoa, milk and flour and mix lightly. Grease a 12-pan muffin tin, or fill with paper cups, and fill with the mixture. Put 1 teaspoon of hazelnut paste onto the centre of each muffin and top with a hazelnut, pressing gently until the nut is half submerged. Bake in an oven preheated to 180°C (350°F) for approximately 25–30 minutes, or until a toothpick inserted into a muffin comes out clean.

Tips and variations

The milk chocolate and hazelnut paste has many uses – it can be rolled in tinfoil and stored in the refrigerator, then sliced into medallions for homemade chocolates. It can be used as a base for other cakes, to fill pain au chocolat and other pastries, or even as a bread spread.

SAFFRON AND RICOTTA MUFFINS

Unusual and aromatic, these muffins are beautiful in colour and provide a welcome change to the usual selection.

Ingredients

10 saffron threads or 1 x sachet saffron
    powder (0.13g)
1 tablespoon water
200g/7oz ricotta cheese
200g/7oz sugar
2 eggs
250g/9oz self-raising flour
2 tablespoons sultanas

Makes 12 muffins

Soak the saffron threads in 1 tablespoon of hot water (or dissolve the saffron powder, if using). Mix the ricotta and sugar with a wooden spoon, then add the eggs and saffron in the water. Lightly mix in the flour and sultanas. Grease a 12-pan muffin tin or fill with paper cups, and fill with the mixture. Bake in an oven preheated to 180°C (350°F) for approximately 25–30 minutes, or until the muffins are well risen and golden in colour.

Tips and variations

If you find the taste of saffron too strong, try the recipe without it. Even simple ricotta muffins taste delicious with the added bonus of containing no butter. The recipe can be used as a low-fat basis for all your muffin variations.

RICOTTA PUFFS

Yet another incredibly easy recipe that will always give good results.

Ingredients

3 x 150g/5oz sheets frozen flaky puff pastry
250g/9oz ricotta cheese
3 tablespoons sugar
3 tablespoons ground almonds
grated zest of 1 lemon
12 red or green glacé cherries (optional)
slivered almonds (optional)
icing sugar for dusting

Makes 12 puffs

Defrost the puff pastry and prick each sheet with a fork to ensure it rises evenly. Divide each sheet into 4 to make a total of 12 pieces. In a bowl mix the ricotta, sugar, ground almonds and lemon zest together. Spoon a little ricotta mixture onto the centre of each piece of pastry and add a glacé cherry, if using. Fold the pastry into triangles or rectangles. Seal the edges, then arrange on a baking tray lined with non-stick baking paper and bake in an oven preheated to 180°C (350°F) for 20 minutes. Sprinkle the tops with icing sugar and slivered almonds, if desired, and return to the oven for a further 10 minutes. Serve cold with tea, coffee or hot chocolate.

Tips and variations

Place a small square of dark chocolate or some candied orange peel in the centre instead of a glacé cherry. Sprinkle plenty of icing sugar directly on the baking paper. It will caramelise into small droplets which, when cold, can be used to decorate the puffs or other cakes and desserts.

POLENTA BISCUITS

I came up with this recipe while trying to finish up some bags of polenta flour. The result was a very thin biscuit with an interesting coarse texture, but a lovely buttery taste.

Ingredients

100g/3½oz unsalted butter
200g/7oz polenta flour (not the
    instant type)
100g/3½oz caster sugar
¼ teaspoon cinnamon
pinch of salt
1 egg

Makes 35–40 biscuits

Melt the butter, then add all the dry ingredients and the egg. Mix with a wooden spoon into a soft paste. Line a baking tray with non-stick baking paper and, taking ½ teaspoons of the mixture at a time, place on the tray, flattening the biscuits into round or oval shapes with the back of the teaspoon. Allow a generous space between the biscuits as they will flatten further during baking. Bake in an oven preheated to 180°C for 10–12 minutes or until the biscuits start to brown at the edges. Allow the biscuits to cool before removing from the baking tray. Store in an airtight container.

Tips and variations

These biscuits are perfect to serve with ice-cream, but are also suitable for a cheeseboard because of their unique taste and texture.

WHITE AND COFFEE MERINGUES

These are two-colour meringues, one side pure white and the other a very light mocha. Because meringues can be very sweet, adding this little bit of coffee will provide a distinctive taste to offset the sweetness.

Ingredients

2 egg whites
6 tablespoons caster sugar
1 teaspoon arrowroot
2 drops lemon juice
1 teaspoon instant coffee powder

Makes 16 meringues

Preheat the oven to 150°C (300°F), ideally on fan bake. Beat the egg whites into stiff peaks. Add the sugar, a spoonful at a time, then the arrowroot and lemon juice, whisking continuously until very stiff. Place spoonfuls of the mixture onto a baking tray lined with non-stick baking paper, making 16 meringues and leaving about 7.5cm (3 inches) between each one. Add the instant coffee powder to the remaining meringue mixture and whisk vigorously. Place a spoonful of the coffee mixture beside each white meringue, making sure that the 2 mixtures are touching. Using your finger, or a teaspoon, curl up the top of each meringue to make a two-colour spiral. Turn the oven down to 50°C (125°F) and bake the meringues for 2 hours. If they are still soft, bake for a further 30 minutes. Once the meringues are hard, turn the oven off and leave them to cool for 1–2 hours, preferably overnight. Serve by themselves or with whipped cream or zabaglione.

Tips and variations

Vary the shapes and try different colours and patterns using a few drops of fruit syrup or food colouring. Meringues look wonderful served on a tray with assorted biscuits and petit fours.

WALNUT BISCUITS WITH CARAMELISED KERNELS

I was very keen to create a biscuit with walnuts, because they are among my favourite nuts. Here is the result.

Ingredients

100g/3½oz walnut halves or pieces
2 eggs, separated
4 tablespoons sugar
1 tablespoon breadcrumbs

CARAMELISED WALNUT KERNELS
2 tablespoons brown sugar
4 tablespoons water
18–20 walnut kernels

Makes 18–20 biscuits

Coarsely grind the walnuts in a food processor. In a bowl beat the egg yolks together with the sugar until pale yellow. Add the ground walnuts and breadcrumbs and fold in. Beat the egg white into stiff peaks. Stir 1 tablespoon of the beaten egg white into the walnut mixture to soften it. Fold in the remaining egg white, then drop teaspoonsful of the mixture onto a baking tray lined with non-stick baking paper to make 18–20 biscuits. Bake in an oven preheated to 180°C (350°F) for just under 10 minutes, turn the oven off, and allow the biscuits to cool in the oven. To prepare the caramelised walnuts, put the brown sugar and water in a saucepan (preferably non-stick) and bring to the boil. Add the whole walnut kernels, one for each biscuit. Stir to coat completely, then allow the caramel to thicken. Place a walnut in the centre of each biscuit and spoon over any leftover caramel. Allow to cool.

Tips and variations

Don't grind the walnuts for too long in the food processor or they will form a paste. If the biscuits become soft after a few days, put them in a hot but turned-off oven to dry.

SHORT PASTRY BISCUIT SELECTION

This is not only the easiest and quickest biscuit recipe, but also the one which provides the most quantity and variety. It is recommended for large parties. Four different biscuits are included in this selection: jam rings, chocolate crescents, hazelnut biscuits and citrus peel biscuits.

Ingredients

1kg/2lb 3oz frozen sweet short crust pastry
100g/3½oz roasted ground hazelnuts
2 tablespoons mixed citrus peel
icing sugar for dusting
2 tablespoons raspberry and/or apricot jam
100g/3½oz dark chocolate, melted

Makes approximately 80 biscuits

Divide the pastry into 4 equal pieces. First prepare the jam rings. Roll out 2 pieces of pastry to 3mm (⅛ inch) thick. Cut out rounds with a 6.5cm (2½ inch) biscuit cutter, then cut a small heart or star shape in the centre of half of the biscuits. Place on a tray and bake in an oven preheated to 180°C for approximately 8 minutes, then allow to cool on the baking tray. Meanwhile roll out the third piece of pastry and cut into crescent shapes (or rectangular, if preferred). Bake as above. Mix the leftover pastry from the jam rings and crescents with the ground hazelnuts, roll into small balls and bake as above. Roll out the fourth piece of pastry and spread the mixed peel evenly over it. Roll into a log shape and cut into 1cm (less than ½ inch) slices. Shape each slice into an oval and bake as above. Sprinkle icing sugar over the hazelnut biscuits and the biscuits with the heart- or star-shaped holes. Spread the whole round biscuits with jam and sandwich together in pairs with an icing-sugared top. Dip half of each crescent biscuit in the melted chocolate. Drizzle any remaining chocolate over the citrus peel biscuits. Serve on a large tray with tea, coffee or a sweet liqueur.

Tips and variations

Pre-rolled pastry is even easier to use for this recipe. Use ground almonds instead of hazelnuts, lemon curd instead of jam, coloured or white icing instead of chocolate, sultanas instead of mixed peel. There are endless variations.

FRUIT VOLS AU VENT

Super easy, quick and colourful, these little vols au vent will look like they are just off the shelves of some famous patisserie. The fruit you select must be firm. *(See photo on page 4)*

Ingredients

2 small peaches
2 black plums
2 yellow plums
8–10 cherries, with stalks
300g/10½oz frozen puff pastry (2 sheets
  of pre-rolled pastry)
caster sugar for dusting

Makes 20–22 pastries

Put the peaches into a pot of boiling water, blanch for 2 minutes, then peel, cut in half and remove the stones. Cut the plums in half and remove the stones. Make an incision at the bottom of each cherry and remove the stone, leaving the stalk on. Roll out the pastry and cut into circles about 2cm (½ inch) larger than the piece of fruit they need to accommodate. Cut the pastry for the larger fruit first, then use the leftover pastry for the cherries. Place the pastry discs on an oven tray lined with non-stick baking paper, place a piece of fruit in the centre of each disc and sprinkle with caster sugar. Place the cherries, stalks up, on their pastry discs at the front of the baking tray. If they roll off their pastry during baking, reposition as quickly as possible. Bake the vols au vent in an oven preheated to 180°C (350°F) for approximately 10–12 minutes or until the pastry is golden and has risen around the fruit. Serve hot or cold.

Tips and variations

For a more substantial dessert fill the stone cavities of the fruit with a mixture of butter, sugar and crushed amaretti biscuits, and serve the vols au vent hot with chocolate sauce. Apricots or grapes can also be used, as can blueberries for tiny vols au vent.

ZALETI

Zaleti are traditional Venetian biscuits, which I love because they are made with corn meal. They are also very buttery, thus quite different from other biscuit recipes in this book. Different sources give different spellings of the name 'Zaleti', but even if it is spelled 'Zaletti', it would still be pronounced the same (this is because there are no strong double consonant sounds in the Venetian accent).

Ingredients

150g/5oz plain flour
150g/5oz fine ground cornmeal
½ teaspoon baking powder
150g/5oz butter, softened
3 egg yolks
100g/3½oz sugar
100g/3½oz sultanas, soaked and drained
1 tablespoon milk, if required
icing sugar for dusting

Makes 35–40 biscuits

Mix the flour, cornmeal and baking powder together in a bowl with the softened butter. Add the egg yolks, sugar and sultanas. Mix into a soft dough, adding a tablespoon of milk if too dry. Divide the dough into 3 pieces and roll out each into a long strip, about 3cm (1¼ inch) thick. Slice into 2cm (¾ inch) thick biscuits and press out into a diamond shape so that each biscuit is about 1cm (less than ½ inch) thick. Place on a baking tray lined with non-stick baking paper and bake in an oven preheated to 180°C for 12 minutes. Allow the biscuits to cool and harden for a few minutes before removing from the baking tray. Serve cold, dusted with icing sugar. Store in an airtight container.

Tips and variations

Some recipes suggest using 2 egg whites rather than 3 yolks, which gives a lighter biscuit. Try them with chocolate chips or candied citrus peel instead of sultanas. Zaleti are a lovely teatime treat and a change from shortbread.

HAZELNUT AND CHOCOLATE FLOWER COOKIES

For those who love hazelnuts and chocolate, here are two cookie recipes merged into one. You can make just one or the other biscuit, or use them together and invent your own shapes.

Ingredients

100g/3½oz roasted hazelnuts
200g/7oz self-raising flour
100g/3½oz sugar
100g/3½oz unsalted butter
2 eggs
1–2 drops hazelnut essence (optional)
1 tablespoon cocoa

Makes 20 large cookies or 40 small biscuits

Finely grind the hazelnuts in a food processor. Mix the flour, sugar and butter together in a bowl until it forms a crumbly texture. Add the eggs, hazelnut essence, if using, and the ground hazelnuts. Mix into a soft sticky dough. Divide the dough in half. Add 1 tablespoon of cocoa to one half of the dough and work in until even in colour. Form each portion into a roll, wrap in cling film, then refrigerate for 30 minutes. To make the biscuits, remove the cling film, cut into 5mm (¼ inch) thick slices and shape into 'flowers', alternating the petals and centres with hazel and chocolate dough. Place on a baking tray lined with non-stick baking paper and bake in an oven preheated to 180°C (350°F) for 12 minutes. Allow the biscuits to cool for 1–2 minutes before removing from the baking tray.

Tips and variations

To roast your own hazelnuts, place them in a tray in a hot oven or in a hot frying pan for 1–2 minutes, then rub them in a clean tea towel while piping hot, and shake off the skins. Hazelnuts can be substituted with almonds. When working with the two biscuit doughs, wash your hands frequently with cold water to prevent the two colours merging as a result of your warm sticky fingers. For a really decadent treat, sandwich the two types of biscuit together either with hazelnut paste *(page 80)*, or unsalted butter and icing sugar with a drop of liqueur.

LAVENDER, ROSE AND ORANGE BLOSSOM TURKISH DELIGHT

When my friend Fiona brought me some homemade Turkish delight I begged her for the recipe! My own version is a long shot from Fiona's original, but I must thank her for having inspired me to reproduce something so exotic at home. Three different flavours are given here.

Ingredients

1 litre/34fl oz water
300g/10½oz sugar
2 teaspoons lemon juice
1 teaspoon pectin powder (optional)
100g/3½oz cornflour
1 tablespoon frozen raspberries
1 tablespoon frozen blueberries
1 teaspoon rose water
1 teaspoon orange blossom water
a few leaves of lavender
lavender petals (optional)
icing sugar and cornflour for dusting

Makes approximately 48 pieces

Boil half the water with the sugar and 1 teaspoon of the lemon juice until a light syrup forms. Put the remaining water in a separate saucepan and stir in the pectin powder, if using, and the cornflour, a spoonful at a time, until it is completely smooth. Bring to the boil. As soon as the cornflour mixture thickens, slowly stir in the syrup and simmer for a further 30 minutes without stirring. Defrost the raspberries and blueberries separately, strain and set the juice aside. Have ready 3 separate plastic containers about 13½ x 10cm (5½ x 4 inches) to set the mixture in. Pour 250ml (8½fl oz) of hot mixture into a measuring jug and return the remaining mixture to the heat to continue simmering. Work very quickly. Add the rose water and raspberry juice to the mixture in the jug, stir, then pour into the first container. To another 250ml (8½fl oz) quantity of the hot mixture add the remaining teaspoon of lemon juice and the orange blossom water, stir, then pour into the second container. Put the lavender leaves in the saucepan with the remaining mixture, add the blueberry juice, stir for a few seconds, then remove the leaves. You can add some lavender petals, if desired. Pour the mixture into the third container. Cool all three flavours for 3–4 hours. Cut each block into 16 pieces, then dust each piece with a mixture of 4 parts cornflour to 1 part icing sugar.

Tips and variations

These Turkish Delights are softer than the commercial ones, but they tend to harden with time. Some classic variations are mint, lemon essence, or chopped pistachio with hazelnut essence. Don't use too much icing sugar to dust the Turkish delight, or it will become soggy.

Cup of Coffee Ice-cream - see recipe on page 101

Ice-creams & Sorbets

For me ice-cream and sorbet represent an ideal dessert, suitable after any kind of meal, and generally liked even by those who are not too keen on sweet things. In summer they are refreshing and light, while in winter they bring respite to a succession of hot dishes. The home ice-cream machine has made life very easy, since almost anything you put into it can became a successful gelato or sorbet. In this chapter I include tips on how to make ices by hand, plus a few recipes which require neither an ice-cream maker nor repetitive stirring, for those of you who are pressed for time yet still want the special flavour of a homemade treat.

RED PLUM SORBET

Use plums with red flesh for a colourful sorbet with a refreshing, slightly tart taste.

Ingredients

12 red plums
500ml/17fl oz water
4 tablespoons sugar

Serves 10

Cut the plums in half and remove the stones. Place in a saucepan with the water and sugar and bring to the boil. Simmer for 1–2 minutes, then remove from the heat and allow to cool. Put the cold plums and their juice into a blender, blend for a few seconds, then pour immediately into an ice-cream maker and churn until ready (about 30 minutes). To make by hand, pour the mixture into a plastic container and place in the freezer. Whisk every 20–30 minutes until the sorbet is ready.

Tips and variations

Thorough blending aerates the mixture. These quantities should make about 1 litre (34fl oz) of sorbet. Add 1 tablespoon of beaten egg white for a softer sorbet. Red Plum Sorbet goes well with Very Vanilla Ice-cream *(page 97)* or it can be served as a palate cleanser between savoury courses.

APRICOT JAM SORBET

Unfinished jars of jam are ideal for making sorbet. Jams are already sweet and often contain pectin, which helps with the sorbet texture. The result is excellent – a strong taste, good colour, even the smell of the fruit is intense. The one problem is that you may get too lazy and make sorbets only from jam, as it is so easy.

Ingredients

200g/7oz apricot jam
500ml/17fl oz water

Serves 6

Put the jam and the water in an electric blender and blend until completely mixed. Pour immediately into an ice-cream maker and churn until ready (about 30 minutes). To make by hand pour into a plastic container and place in the freezer. Whisk every 20–30 minutes until the sorbet is ready.

Tips and variations

Any jam can be used. Raspberry jam with pectin is particularly good, as it is otherwise difficult to create a thick sorbet with the berries themselves. Search for unusual jams in delicatessen stores: fig, persimmon and gooseberries, for example, can create unusual ices. Increasing the amount of jam will give more flavour, but also more sugar and possibly a jam taste that will give away your secret.

HAZELNUT GELATO WITH FRANGELICO LIQUEUR

Frangelico is a sweet Italian liqueur with an intense hazelnut perfume. If unavailable, use Amaretto or Galliano liqueur with a few drops of hazelnut essence.

Ingredients

100g/3^1/$_2$oz hazelnuts, shelled
1 egg, separated
4 tablespoons sugar
200ml/7fl oz whipping cream
2 tablespoons Frangelico liqueur

Serves 4–6

Place the hazelnuts in a hot oven or hot frying pan for 1–2 minutes to roast. Transfer to a tea towel while piping hot and shake off the skins. Place the cleaned nuts in a food processor and grind very finely. Half fill a medium saucepan with warm water and set over a medium heat. Whisk the egg yolk together with 3 tablespoons of the sugar and half the cream in a small bowl. Set the bowl over the saucepan of simmering water and slowly add the ground hazelnuts, stirring continuously. Once the egg mixture has thickened, remove from the heat and cool, stirring occasionally, then add the liqueur in 2 stages. In a separate bowl whip the remaining cream and fold into the egg mixture, then pour immediately into an ice-cream maker. In another bowl beat the egg white into stiff peaks, adding the remaining tablespoon of sugar towards the end. When the gelato is almost ready, add the beaten egg white and churn for a further 5 minutes. To make by hand, pour the mixture into a plastic container and place in the freezer. Whisk every 20–30 minutes, adding the beaten egg white once the gelato starts to solidify. Serve topped with crushed toasted hazelnuts, if desired.

Tips and variations

For an easy vanilla ice-cream follow the same method, adding the seeds of 1 vanilla pod instead of hazelnuts, and omitting the liqueur. For a coffee gelato substitute the nuts with 1 teaspoon of instant coffee, and the Frangelico with a coffee liqueur. Hazelnut Gelato goes well with Very Vanilla Ice-cream (see opposite) and Rich Chocolate Ice-cream (page 101).

VERY VANILLA ICE-CREAM

Vanilla must be the world's best known and most loved ice-cream flavour. It is certainly one of my favourites. And if you still remember old-fashioned vanilla ices, you will certainly notice the lack of taste that many commercial ice-creams have today, mainly due to the use of synthetic vanilla essence. It's the reason why I like to see the vanilla seeds in this ice-cream – and plenty of them, too – as proof that it is truly a very vanilla ice.

Ingredients

3 egg yolks
4 tablespoons sugar
250ml/8½fl oz milk, preferably full cream
1 vanilla pod
100ml/3½fl oz whipping cream
1 egg white

Serves 6

■ Half-fill a medium saucepan with warm water and set over a medium heat. In a bowl beat the egg yolks together with 3 tablespoons of the sugar. Slit open the vanilla pod and add it with its seeds and the milk to the egg mixture. Set the bowl over the saucepan of simmering water and simmer, stirring occasionally, until the mixture thickens. Allow to cool. In a separate bowl whip the cream until stiff. In another bowl whip the egg white with the remaining tablespoon of sugar. Remove the vanilla pod from the egg mixture, then fold in the whipped cream and beaten egg white. Pour into an ice-cream maker and churn until ready (approximately 30 minutes). If making by hand, pour the mixture into a plastic container and stir frequently (every 20–30 minutes) to prevent it from freezing into a solid block. Serve as desired.

Tips and variations

Variations to this ice-cream are limited only by your imagination. Add 1–2 tablespoons of Baileys or other liqueur to the almost-frozen mixture. Add chopped nuts or chocolate chips, glacé cherries or apples, crushed cookies, pralines, rum and raisins . . . whatever your heart and palate dictate. This versatile ice-cream can be served with almost anything.

PEACHES AND CREAM ICE

Lovely, summery and evocative of an idyllic countryside, this ice-cream makes a delicious dessert served with fresh raspberries.

Ingredients

1 egg white
3 tablespoons caster sugar
300ml/10fl oz whipping cream
1 drop vanilla essence
4 large ripe peaches

Serves 4–6

Whip the egg white and 2 tablespoons of the caster sugar into stiff peaks. In a separate bowl whip the cream. Fold in the beaten egg white and vanilla essence. Set the ice-cream machine in motion and pour in the egg and cream mixture. Peel and stone the peaches and cut into thin slices directly into a bowl to catch all the juice. Add the remaining tablespoon of caster sugar and mash the peaches lightly with a spoon. Pour into the ice-cream mixture and churn until ready (about 30 minutes). Serve, preferably immediately, while the ice-cream is still soft, with lots of fresh raspberries.

Tips and variations

Follow the same method for strawberry, cherry, mango, apricot or nectarine ices with cream. Chocolate chips can be added.

FROZEN YOGHURT WITH HONEY AND PISTACHIO NUTS

An easy recipe that is perfect for those who like the tangy taste of yoghurt. If you don't have an ice-cream maker, simply pour the mixture into ice block moulds and wait.

Ingredients

1 tablespoon pistachio nuts, shelled
1 tablespoon sugar
500ml/17fl oz plain full-fat yoghurt,
    preferably Greek-style
4–5 tablespoons liquid honey
nuts and honey to serve

Serves 4–6

Coarsely grind the pistachio nuts with the sugar in a pestle and mortar, leaving a few bigger pieces. Blend the yoghurt with the honey and set aside for a few minutes until the honey is fully dissolved. Mix in the ground pistachio nuts, pour into an ice-cream machine and churn until ready. Serve topped with more liquid honey and crushed pistachio nuts, if desired.

Tips and variations

Any flavoured full-fat yoghurt can be put into an ice-cream machine or ice block moulds, as it freezes well. Pistachio nuts can be substituted with toasted hazelnuts or fresh berries, and the honey with maple syrup.

HONEYDEW AND WATERMELON GRANITA

Two delicious granite, which can be made separately, but are at their best when served together. You don't need an ice-cream maker for these.

Ingredients

HONEYDEW GRANITA
300g/10½oz honeydew melon, peeled and deseeded
100g/3½oz sugar
200ml/7fl oz water

WATERMELON GRANITA
600g/1lb 2oz watermelon, peeled and deseeded
100g/3½oz sugar

Serves 8 as a dessert, 16 as an interlude between courses

Blend the honeydew melon with the sugar and water. Pour into a plastic container with a lid and freeze. Blend the watermelon and sugar and put into a separate container and freeze. Stir the two granite frequently (every 20–30 minutes) to prevent them from becoming a solid block of ice, but allowing the ice crystals to form naturally. Scoop into tall glasses or melon shells and serve.

Tips and variations

Use three varieties of melon (yellow, orange and green) for a triple granita. Add vodka to the watermelon or rum to the honeydew, but not both.

SEMIFREDDO WITH AMARETTO AND CHOCOLATE

Semifreddo is a type of ice-cream that requires neither an ice-cream maker nor stirring by hand. The important thing is to whip all the ingredients well.

Ingredients

10 amaretti biscuits
50g/2oz dark chocolate
3 eggs, separated
3 tablespoons sugar
1 tablespoon Amaretto liqueur
300ml/10fl oz whipping cream
amaretti biscuits and whipped cream to serve (optional)

Serves 8

Line a 23 x 13cm (9 x 5 inch) loaf tin with cling film and place in the freezer. Crush the amaretti biscuits into small crumbs. Chop the chocolate into small pieces, mix with the crushed biscuits and place in the freezer. Beat the egg yolks together with the sugar until pale yellow and foamy. Add the Amaretto and continue beating. In a separate bowl whip the cream until stiff, then fold into the egg mixture. Fold in the crushed biscuit mixture. In another bowl, beat the egg whites into stiff peaks and fold into the mixture. Pour immediately into the loaf tin and freeze for at least 4 hours. Before serving leave the semifreddo to thaw for a few minutes, then turn onto a serving dish, peel off the cling film and cut into 8 slices. Serve accompanied with a few whole amaretti biscuits and some whipped cream, if desired.

Tips and variations

Substitute the Amaretto liqueur with dark rum and the amaretti biscuits and chocolate with raisins for a delicious rum and raisin semifreddo.

CUP OF COFFEE ICE-CREAM

A chance to serve coffee and dessert at the same time! Start the ice-cream maker while you are enjoying your main dish, then serve this ice-cream immediately, like a freshly brewed cup of coffee.

Ingredients

6 tablespoons sugar
300ml/10fl oz boiling water
150ml/5fl oz espresso coffee
1 tablespoon coffee liqueur (optional)
1 egg white
1 tablespoon icing sugar
whipped cream and cinnamon stick
    to serve (optional)

Serves 8

Dissolve the sugar in the boiling water, then allow to cool. Add the coffee if using and the liqueur, and pour into the ice-cream maker. Beat the egg white and the icing sugar into stiff peaks. When the ice-cream starts to solidify add the egg white. Once the ice-cream is ready (after about 30 minutes), scoop it into 8 coffee cups, decorate each with whipped cream and a cinnamon stick, if desired, and serve on a saucer with a teaspoon. To make by hand, pour the mixture into a plastic container and place in the freezer. Whisk every 20–30 minutes until the ice-cream is ready, adding the beaten egg white once the ice-cream starts to solidify.

Tips and variations

The same method can be used to make a 'cup of cocoa' ice-cream. Use drinking cocoa powder, ideally Dutch, instead of coffee. The strength of both coffee and cocoa can be varied according to taste.

RICH CHOCOLATE ICE-CREAM

A chocolate ice-cream should be intense and velvety, akin to the taste you expect from a chocolate truffle. This recipe serves 4, but the quantities can easily be doubled or tripled.

Ingredients

1 egg yolk
1 tablespoon sugar
100ml/3½fl oz milk (preferably full cream)
100g/3½oz dark chocolate
2 egg whites

Serves 4

Put the egg yolk and the sugar in a heavy-based saucepan and whisk. Over a very low heat, stir in the milk. Break the chocolate into the mixture and stir continuously until the chocolate melts. Simmer for 1–2 minutes, then allow to cool, stirring occasionally. In a separate bowl, beat the egg whites into stiff peaks, then fold gently into the chocolate sauce. Pour into an ice-cream maker and churn until ready (approximately 30 minutes). If making by hand, pour the mixture into a plastic container and stir frequently (every 20–30 minutes) to prevent it from freezing into a solid block. The large quantity of chocolate will help keep the mixture creamy. Serve by itself or with fresh raspberries and cream.

Tips and variations

Add ground hazelnuts for an Italian gianduia-style ice-cream, or some espresso coffee for a more intense flavour. Rich chocolate Ice-cream goes well with Very Vanilla Ice-cream (page 97), Hazelnut Gelato (page 96) or Coconut Ice-cream (page 106).

EASY MANGO KULFI

Kulfi is a traditional Indian ice-cream, and this version must be the simplest of all. There are just two ingredients, and no need for an ice-cream machine or stirring. The result is a very sweet but delicate ice-cream, which can be easily 'spiced up' by the addition of half a teaspoon of ground cardamom, or a teaspoon of rose water.

Ingredients

1 x 395g (13oz) can sweetened
   condensed milk
1 x 400g (13oz) can mango in syrup

Serves 8

Empty the contents of the two cans into a blender and blend until frothy. The more air in the mixture, the better the results. Pour immediately into 8 individual metal pastry cones or moulds or into a 20cm (8 inch) round tin. Place immediately in the freezer for at least 4 hours. Before serving tip the moulds onto individual serving plates and wrap in a warm tea towel. The kulfi should slip out easily. If frozen in a round tin, cut into slices or use an ice-cream scoop. Serve immediately.

Tips and variations

The kulfi melts quickly, so don't take it out of the freezer too far in advance of serving. It is perfect after a Indian meal, but if you find it too sweet, use unsweetened condensed milk, or fresh mangos. It goes well with strawberries and other berries, and can be decorated with edible silver paper, available in Indian food stores or cake stores. To make your own kulfi moulds, roll some non-stick baking paper into cone shapes, and place them inside waffle ice-cream cones. Fill with kulfi mixture, place upright in a tall glass and freeze. Before serving simply empty the waffle cones and peel the paper off.

STRAWBERRY SORBET

If you are lucky enough to live where there are wild strawberries, this sorbet will acquire a perfume and taste equal to none. But even commercially grown strawberries can develop a great flavour when marinated with lemon and sugar, as in this recipe.

Ingredients

20 strawberries, approximately
3 tablespoons sugar
juice of ½ lemon
200ml/7fl oz water
mint leaves and fresh blueberries to decorate (optional)

Serves 4–6

Lightly rinse and dry the strawberries. Set some aside for decoration, then halve or quarter the larger ones. Place in a bowl, then add the sugar and lemon juice. Leave to marinate for 3–4 hours, preferably overnight, stirring occasionally. Put the strawberries and their juice in a blender with the water and blend until light and foamy. Pour the mixture into an ice-cream maker and churn until ready (approximately 30 minutes). If making by hand, pour the mixture into a plastic container and stir frequently (every 20–30 minutes) to prevent it from freezing into a solid block. Serve immediately, decorated with the whole strawberries, a few mint leaves and fresh blueberries.

Tips and variations

Substitute the lemon juice with 1 tablespoon of balsamic vinegar for a more intense flavour. Strawberry Sorbet goes well with Lemon Sorbet *(see opposite)*. Use the same method to make sorbet with raspberries, blueberries, blackberries or mixed berry fruit. Add a drop of vodka, if desired. The marinated strawberries are a wonderful dessert in their own right. In Italy they are known as *fragole al limone*. Try them by themselves or with a little cream.

GRANNY SMITH APPLE SORBET

This sorbet is fragrant, refreshing and has a beautiful light pistachio colour. Serve this as you would the Lemon Sorbet *(see opposite)* either as a dessert or as a palate cleanser between savoury dishes.

Ingredients

4 tablespoons sugar
250ml/8½fl oz boiling water
1 tablespoon lemon juice
500g/1lb 2oz Granny Smith apples, cored but not peeled

Serves 6 as a dessert, 12 as an interlude between courses

Dissolve the sugar in the boiling water, add the lemon juice and allow to cool before pouring into a blender. Slice the cored apples into the lemon water to prevent them turning brown. Blend into a thick, foamy shake (in 2 stages, if necessary) and pour immediately into an ice-cream maker until ready (approximately 20–30 minutes). To make by hand, pour the mixture into a plastic container and place in the freezer. Whisk every 20–30 minutes until the sorbet is ready. Decorate with mint leaves or cinnamon sticks, if desired.

Tips and variations

Green apples give the best taste to my mind, but other apples are also suitable. Always retain the peel for taste and colour – golden delicious for yellow sorbet and red apples for pink.

LEMON SORBET WITH LIMONCINO LIQUEUR

Nothing is more refreshing on a hot summer's day than a lemon sorbet, and no dessert is lighter after a heavy meal, or has the same capacity to cleanse the palate from strong flavours. This is why sorbet is served as an interlude between different dishes, usually fish and meat.

Ingredients

4 lemons
4 tablespoons white sugar
4 tablespoons icing sugar
500ml/17fl oz water
50ml/2fl oz Limoncino liqueur

Serves 8

Squeeze the juice from the lemons and pour into a saucepan. Add the white sugar, icing sugar and water and bring to the boil. Simmer and stir until the sugar has dissolved. Remove from the heat and allow to cool. Put in an ice-cream maker and churn. When the sorbet starts to solidify add the liqueur. Best served immediately or store in the freezer for later use.

Tips and variations

Generally, sorbets take longer to make in an ice-cream maker than dairy ice-creams. Use more Limoncino if you wish, but remember that too much alcohol will prevent the sorbet from freezing. Lemon and vodka taste great too. Freeze the squeezed lemon halves and fill them with sorbet. Use large lemons with thick skin and lots of leaves. Freeze with the leaves. Lemon Sorbet goes well with Strawberry Sorbet (see opposite). Use the same method to make lime, orange, grapefruit and other citrus sorbets, but reduce or increase the quantity of water according to the amount of juice used.

COCONUT ICE-CREAM

Perfectly white and creamy, this ice-cream is the ideal accompaniment for fruit salads and pies, especially for those who like something a little different in taste, or are intolerant to dairy products, but who may still crave that velvety, cream-like texture.

Ingredients

1 x 400ml (13fl oz) can coconut cream
5 tablespoons caster sugar
1 egg white

Serves 4–6

Blend the coconut cream with 1 tablespoon of the caster sugar until it has the consistency of a milkshake. Pour into an ice-cream maker and churn. Whip the egg whites into stiff peaks, add the remaining 4 tablespoons of caster sugar, a spoonful at a time, and pour into the ice-cream maker once the ice-cream starts to solidify (about 20–30 minutes). Serve by itself, with berries or with Rich Chocolate Ice-cream (page 101). To make by hand, pour into a plastic container and place in the freezer. Whisk every 20–30 minutes until the ice-cream is ready, adding the beaten egg white once the ice-cream starts to solidify.

Tips and variations

Add 1 tablespoon of Malibu liqueur or Amaretto (this may tint the pure whiteness of the ice-cream), or Blue Curaçao, for a pale blue hue. Serve in a coconut shell. Coconut ice-cream goes well with Banana Fruit Salad (page 115) or with fresh blackberries.

PINEAPPLE AND VODKA ICE-CREAM

A tangy and tempting dessert. Serve this ice-cream in the hollowed pineapple – it looks fantastic.

Ingredients

4 tablespoons white sugar
200ml/7fl oz boiling water
1 large pineapple
50ml/2fl oz vodka
1 egg white
1 tablespoon icing sugar
vanilla pods or cherries to
    decorate (optional)

Serves 8

Dissolve the sugar in the boiling water and allow to cool. Working over a large bowl to save as much juice as possible, cut the top off the pineapple. Using a small knife, cut around the inside of the fruit, leaving 1.5cm ($\frac{1}{2}$ inch) around the sides. Remove the flesh and place in the bowl. Cut the base of the pineapple shell if necessary to make it stand upright, and place with the top in the freezer for later use. Cut the pineapple flesh into small pieces, discarding the core, and mix in a blender for a few seconds with the cooled water and the vodka. In a bowl beat the egg white and the icing sugar into stiff peaks.

Pour the pineapple mixture into an ice-cream maker and churn, adding the beaten egg white as soon as the ice-cream starts to solidify. If making the ice-cream by hand, pour the pineapple mixture into a plastic container and freeze for 30 minutes, then whisk. Repeat 3 times, adding the beaten egg white at the final whisking. To serve, place the frozen pineapple case on a serving plate. Fill with full scoops of ice-cream. Put the pineapple top on, adjusting it over the scoops of ice-cream, which should overflow their natural container. Decorate with vanilla pods or fresh cherries, if desired.

Tips and variations

A pineapple corer, which works like a corkscrew, makes removing the pineapple flesh much easier. If handmade ice-cream turns into a block of ice, break it into smaller pieces and whisk with an electric beater. Substitute vodka with rum for a Caribbean version. Canned pineapple can also be used for a much sweeter taste.

BANANA AND KIWI GOLD ICE-CREAM

This could qualify as a sorbet because of the absence of dairy products and eggs, but the banana gives it more of an ice-cream texture.

Ingredients

2 tablespoons sugar
250ml/8½fl oz boiling water
1–2 drops lemon juice
4 yellow kiwifruit, peeled
1 banana, peeled

Serves 6

■ Dissolve the sugar in the boiling water, add the lemon juice, then allow it to cool. In a blender mix the yellow kiwifruit with the banana and the cooled sweetened water until it forms a frothy shake. Pour immediately into an ice-cream maker and churn until the ice-cream is ready (about 30 minutes). Serve accompanied by thin slices of kiwifruit, if desired. To make by hand, pour into a plastic container and place in the freezer. Whisk every 20–30 minutes until the ice-cream is ready.

Tips and variations

You can use green kiwifruit, but the yellow type is sweeter and requires less sugar. Adjust the sugar according to taste. Add a drop of liqueur, if desired. This ice-cream goes well with any berry ice-cream.

G&T AND CUBA LIBRE ICE BLOCKS

More of an idea than a recipe, but they are just so cool, and will make your next summer party something everybody will remember!

Ingredients

G&T ICE BLOCK
gin
tonic water
2 slices of lime per ice block

CUBA LIBRE ICE BLOCK
rum
coke

■ Make up as many gin and tonics or cuba libres as required without too much alcohol, otherwise they won't freeze. Leave until the drinks are flat, then pour them into individual ice-block moulds, inserting 2 lime slices in each gin and tonic mould. Don't fill the moulds to the top, as the ice blocks expand as they freeze. Place in the freezer until set and serve instead of cocktails on a hot summer day.

Tips and variations

Experiment with your favourite cocktails and have a selection ready. This is an excellent way to finish up mixer bottles that have lost their fizz.

Dried Fruit with Chocolate and Marzipan - see recipe on page 121

Fruit Fancies

For centuries, people have favoured fruit as the ideal way to end a main meal. Quite apart from eating it raw, there are so many wonderful ways in which fruit can be cooked and combined with other delicious ingredients. And as we all know, fruit contains a large variety of vitamins to keep us healthy. But if we want to make the most of what fruit has to offer us, we should really eat it separately from main meals. This is because it can actually slow the digestive process. But as for all sweet things, the occasional indulgence does no harm.

EXOTIC FRUIT SALAD

Tropical fruit is the ideal ending for an exotic meal, especially one featuring spices. In this recipe I have included nata de coco, a kind of jelly derived from coconut that originated in the Philippines. It is available in most Asian food stores and comes cut into cubes and preserved in a glass jar with syrup.

Ingredients

100ml/3½fl oz chilled water
100ml/3½fl oz guava or pineapple juice
1–2 drops lemon juice
1 can lychees in syrup
1 jar nata de coco (optional)
2 bananas
1 papaya
1 mango
2 passionfruit

Serves 8

Put the water, fruit juice and lemon juice in a large fruit salad bowl, add the lychees and syrup, and the nata de coco and syrup, if using. Peel and slice the bananas and add to the fruit mixture. Peel the papaya and mango, cut them into 2cm (1 inch) squares and add to the fruit mixture. Stir in the pulp and seeds of the passionfruit. Refrigerate for 2 hours and serve with plenty of the juice.

Tips and variations

Any tropical fruit works well with this recipe, and the nata de coco adds texture and curiosity to this dessert. For a special occasion serve in glass tumblers decorated with orchids, frangipani or other exotic flowers.

ICY ITALIAN FRUIT SALAD

Fruit salad is often improvised with whatever fruit is at hand. The quantities in this recipe should be taken as a guideline. What distinguishes this dessert is the strawberry ice cubes, which are unusual and refreshing. This salad is best if the fruit is prepared shortly before serving.

Ingredients

12 strawberries
water
juice of 1 lemon
2 yellow peaches
2 firm pears
1 slice watermelon
2 nectarines
2 kiwifruit
12 cherries with stalks

Serves 8–10

Lightly rinse the strawberries and set a few aside for serving. Halve the remaining strawberries. Place the halved berries in an empty ice-tray, one in each compartment, then cover with water and freeze. Put the lemon juice in a large serving bowl. Peel the peaches and pears, cut into 2cm (1 inch) squares and toss in the lemon juice. Peel the watermelon, remove as many seeds as possible, add to the fruit bowl and toss. Wash and slice the nectarines, peel and slice the kiwifruit and toss both with the other fruit. Add the cherries with their stalks and the whole strawberries. Add the strawberry ice cubes and toss with the other fruit. Serve immediately.

Tips and variations

Try serving this fruit salad in the hollowed-out shell of half a watermelon or in an ice bowl, placed on a serving plate decorated with leaves and flowers.

MELON STRIPS WITH HONEY

This is a super-stylish way of serving melon, but bear in mind that only orange-fleshed melons (netted or musk varieties) should be used, providing a contrast with the green peel when served.

Ingredients

1 melon
3 teaspoons liquid honey
1 tablespoon lemon juice
crushed ice to serve

Serves 6

Peel the rougher outer skin of the melon with a potato or vegetable peeler, taking care not to remove the green inner peel. Cut the melon in two and remove all the seeds. Using a large knife, carefully slice the melon into very thin strips. Place on a dish, drizzle with the honey and lemon juice, and refrigerate for 1–2 hours. Before serving roll each melon slice into a cone shape and arrange on a tray filled with crushed ice. Serve immediately.

Tips and variations

Use port instead of lemon juice. Melon is good by itself, or it can be accompanied with a variety of fruit such as strawberries, cherries and fresh lychees.

POMEGRANATES WITH ORANGE INFUSION

Splendid in colour and freshness, this easy fruit dessert is sure to please the most sophisticated palates.

Ingredients

3 pomegranates
1 tablespoon sugar
juice of 1 orange
1–2 drops orange blossom water (optional)
orange zest to decorate
ice cubes to serve (optional)

Serves 4

Cut the pomegranates over a bowl. Remove the seeds and discard all the white membrane and skin, collecting all the juice in the bowl. Add the sugar, orange juice and orange blossom water, if using. Refrigerate for 1–2 hours to allow the fruit to absorb the syrup. Decorate with long strips of orange zest. Serve chilled with a few ice cubes, if desired.

Tips and variations

Substitute orange juice with lemon or lime juice. Serve accompanied with crème fraîche or mascarpone. Rose water can be used instead of orange blossom water.

BALSAMIC APPLE SKEWERS

Aromatic and crunchy, these apple skewers are easy to make and are ideal for parties and buffets. The best balsamic vinegar to use is Aceto Balsamico di Modena – not necessarily an expensive 60-year-old one, just any that is authentic and therefore not acidic.

Ingredients

200ml/7fl oz water
4 tablespoons sugar
2 tablespoons balsamic vinegar
6 apples (2 red, 2 green and 2 yellow)

Makes 12 skewers

Boil the water with the sugar and balsamic vinegar for a few minutes until a light syrup forms, then allow to cool to body temperature. Meanwhile wash and core the apples, but do not peel. Cut each apple into 6 slices, then each slice into 3 pieces. As you cut, drop the pieces into the syrup. When all the apples have been cut and sliced, thread each piece onto a skewer, alternating the colours (red, yellow, green). Each skewer should hold 6 pieces of apple. Pour the remaining syrup into a dipping bowl to accompany the apple skewers.

Tips and variations

Use half a melon as a 'pin cushion' to display the apple skewers. Substitute or alternate apple pieces with large strawberries.

BANANA FRUIT SALAD

Apart from berry fruit, a fruit salad made from only one type of fruit generally doesn't sound too appetising. But try this. It is perfect for when you have unexpected guests, need a dessert in a hurry and have a bunch of bananas at hand.

Ingredients

1 tablespoon sugar
1–2 drops lemon juice
1 litre/34fl oz apple juice
1 cinnamon stick (optional)
2 tablespoons rum (optional)
4 bananas, peeled

Serves 6

In a large serving bowl dissolve the sugar in the lemon juice. Add the apple juice, cinnamon stick and rum, if using. Slice the bananas directly into the bowl, stirring occasionally to ensure they are completely covered with juice. Refrigerate preferably for 1–2 hours before serving.

Tips and variations

Pear and pineapple juice are also suitable, as is the addition of grappa or your favourite liqueur. This fruit salad goes well with Very Vanilla Ice-cream *(page 97)* or Coconut Ice-cream *(page 106)*, or as a base for more complex fruit salads. Make a large bowlful of this salad for a buffet meal. It will look and taste interesting alongside other types of fruit and desserts.

STRAWBERRIES WITH RED WINE

Tiny wild strawberries are best for this unusual dessert, but as they are difficult to find, I use ripe, juicy garden strawberries. Of course you don't need to waste your best red wine on this recipe – most light table wines will do, as will that unfinished bottle taking up space on the kitchen bench.

Ingredients

500g/1lb 2oz ripe strawberries, hulled
3 teaspoons sugar
500ml/17fl oz light red wine
1 cinnamon stick (optional)

Serves 10

Wash and cut the strawberries into small pieces and place in a serving bowl with the sugar. Stir, cover and leave for 1 hour at room temperature. Add the wine and cinnamon stick, refrigerate and leave to marinate for 1–2 hours before serving, ideally in attractive red wine glasses.

Tips and variations

Add orange zest before serving for flavour and colour. Follow the same recipe to make a strawberry sangria, but double the quantity of red wine, add an equal quantity of lemonade, and then enough rum to suit your taste. Unpeeled apple and orange segments can also be added. In autumn, when figs are in season, use them instead of strawberries: peel the figs with a small knife, cut in half and marinate as for the strawberries. Serve with whipped cream or mascarpone.

FIGS WITH HONEY AND ALMONDS

This is a great way to serve figs. Their natural sweetness is further enhanced by the honey. They are extra good served with a cheese board.

Ingredients

6 fresh firm figs
3 teaspoons liquid honey
1 tablespoon slivered almonds

Serves 4

Cut the figs in half lengthwise and place them cut side up on a serving plate. Place a small amount of honey in the centre of each fig. Cover and set aside for 1–2 hours. Before serving sprinkle each half with slivered almonds.

Tips and variations

If you use purple figs you can substitute the almonds with coarsely chopped pistachio nuts. Maple syrup instead of honey is another tasty variation.

FRUIT OF THE FOREST IN BALSAMIC JELLY WITH MANGO IN BALSAMIC SAUCE

Balsamic vinegar is a fantastic ingredient and very much in vogue at the moment.

Ingredients

JELLY
300ml/10fl oz water
3 tablespoons sugar
½ teaspoon agar agar
1 tablespoon balsamic vinegar
200g/7oz frozen mixed berries

MANGO AND SAUCE
150ml/5fl oz water
3 tablespoons sugar
1 tablespoon balsamic vinegar
2 ripe mangoes

Serves 6

To make the jelly, put the water, sugar and agar agar in a saucepan and bring to the boil. When the sugar is dissolved add the balsamic vinegar and frozen berries. Return to the boil, then pour immediately into 6 individual jelly moulds or ramekins and allow to set (1–2 hours). To prepare the sauce, boil the water with the sugar and balsamic vinegar for 1–2 minutes and keep warm. Peel and slice the mangoes and divide equally between 6 serving plates. Turn the jellies onto the serving plates and pour over the warm balsamic sauce. Serve immediately.

Tips and variations

If you over-boil the fruit it will disintegrate – whole berries are better in the jelly. Substitute the berries with peaches and the mango with strawberries for a complete contrast in colour and taste. For another recipe using balsamic vinegar, see Balsamic Apple Skewers (page 115).

WARM PEACHES WITH AMARETTO SAUCE

Use large, ripe, preferably yellow peaches for this delightful warm fruit dessert.

Ingredients

4 peaches
10–15g/½oz unsalted butter
2 tablespoons sugar
4 tablespoons Amaretto liqueur
whipped cream or crème anglaise to serve

Serves 4

Blanch the peaches in boiling water for 1 minute. Peel, then cut each one into 6 slices and remove the stones. In a frying pan (preferably non-stick) melt the butter over a low heat, then add the peach slices, sugar and 1 tablespoon of Amaretto. Stir the peaches with a wooden spoon until they start to soften. Divide between 4 dessert plates. Return the frying pan to the heat and add the remaining 3 tablespoons of Amaretto. Simmer for a few seconds while stirring, then pour the liquid over the peaches. Serve immediately with whipped cream or crème anglaise, if desired.

Tips and variations

Substitute Amaretto with brandy or peach liqueur. Top with grated dark chocolate. When peaches are not in season use apples or pears. They will need a little longer to cook.

STRAWBERRIES AND CREAM BRÛLÉE

An amazing variation on the standard strawberries and cream, which will surprise your guests. As a bonus, this recipe is unbelievably easy.

Ingredients

250g/9oz strawberries (preferably
    small ones), hulled
4 teaspoons sweet liqueur (optional)
100ml/3½fl oz whipping cream
1 teaspoon icing sugar
8 teaspoons brown (or Moscovado) sugar

Serves 4

Lightly rinse the strawberries and dry them with kitchen paper. Leave the smallest strawberries whole, cut the bigger ones into 2–3 pieces, then divide them between 4 small ramekins or crème brûlée dishes. Add 1 teaspoon of liqueur to each ramekin, if desired. Whip the cream with the icing sugar. Cover the strawberries with the whipped cream, gently banging the dishes on the working surface to remove all air bubbles. Cover each ramekin with cling film and place in the freezer for approximately 30 minutes. Remove from the freezer and spoon 2 teaspoons of brown sugar evenly over each dessert and place under a hot grill for 1–2 minutes. When the sugar changes colour and becomes shiny, remove the ramekins from under the grill, cool at room temperature for a few minutes, then refrigerate. Serve within 1–2 hours to ensure the top remains crunchy.

Tips and variations

The longer you leave this dessert after grilling, the softer the sugar will become. Avoid using over-ripe strawberries and dry them properly after rinsing to prevent liquid forming at the bottom of the dessert. Raspberries are also suitable.

DRIED FRUIT WITH CHOCOLATE AND MARZIPAN

Offer a tray of these luxurious and decadent delights with coffee as the finale for an important meal or at a formal Christmas party. The marzipan in this recipe is made with vanilla icing sugar, which is simply icing sugar stored in a jar with a vanilla pod.

Ingredients

MARZIPAN
200g/7oz unblanched almonds
100g/3½oz vanilla icing sugar
1 drop red food colouring
1 drop green food colouring

8 fresh dates
6 tablespoons water
2 tablespoons sugar
8 blanched almonds
8 pecan nuts, shelled
8 pistachio nuts, shelled
8 dried apricots
50 g / 2 oz dark chocolate
8 dried figs

Makes 48 pieces

■ To make the marzipan, blanch the almonds in boiling water for a few minutes and remove the skins. Grind the almonds in a food processor until they form a paste. Put the almond paste in a bowl and add the vanilla icing sugar. Work the mixture with your fingers until smooth, then turn the marzipan onto a marble bench or a plastic chopping board and divide into 4 equal portions. Roll 1 portion out to a thickness of about 2cm (under 1 inch) and cut into 8 smaller pieces. Shape each piece into a small ball, flatten slightly and set aside. Add 1 drop of red food colouring to the second portion of marzipan and repeat as above to form 8 small balls. Add 1 drop of green food colouring to the third portion of marzipan, and repeat as above. Open the dates and remove the stones. Stuff the dates with the remaining portion of marzipan. Put the water and sugar into a saucepan and bring to the boil. Add the blanched almonds, pecan nuts and pistachio nuts and simmer for 1–2 minutes. Using a pair of tweezers, place the nuts on top of the marzipan balls – almonds on the pink, pistachio on the green, and pecan on the plain marzipan. Break the chocolate into the syrup in the saucepan and simmer until the chocolate has melted. Coat half of each dried apricot with the chocolate and put aside on a non-stick surface to set. Use the remaining chocolate to partly coat the dried figs. Arrange all the fruit and marzipan on a large tray and serve.

Tips and variations

Homemade marzipan is in a league of its own, but if you are pressed for time, use bought marzipan. Don't make marzipan with ground almonds as they are too dry. Use your imagination and create your own marzipan shapes and sweets.

GLOSSARY

AGAR AGAR: a setting agent derived from seaweed. Usually found in powder or strip form in Asian stores, it can be used instead of gelatine, with the advantage that it is less expensive, sets at room temperature, and is a good source of vegetable fibre.

AMARETTI BISCUITS: Italian macaroon biscuits made with bitter almonds.

AMARETTO LIQUEUR: Sweet Italian liqueur made with bitter almonds.

ARROWROOT: a thickener of plant origin (obtained from the rhizomes, or underground stems). Widely used in gluten-free recipes.

COINTREAU: Sweet French liqueur made with sweet and bitter oranges.

FRANGELICO: Sweet Italian liqueur made with hazelnuts.

GALLIANO: Sweet Italian liqueur widely used in cocktails and, sometimes, desserts.

GRAND MARNIER: Sweet French liqueur made with oranges and widely used in desserts.

GRAPPA: Italian distillate made from the leftover skins, pips and stalks of grapes, after wine has been made. Highly alcoholic, but excellent for desserts.

LIMONCINO: Sweet Italian liqueur with a strong lemon taste (also known as Limoncello).

MASCARPONE: Soft fresh Italian cheese made from cream coagulated with citric acid. Widely used for desserts, and sometimes savoury dishes.

NATA DE COCO: A jelly derived from the coconut plant, widely available in Asian stores, already cubed and preserved in syrup.

RICOTTA: Italian curd cheese made as a by-product from the whey of several cow and ewe's cheeses. It can be used raw or cooked in many desserts as well as savoury dishes.

SAMBUCA: Sweet Italian aniseed liqueur, usually drunk as a digestive, or used for desserts.

SASSOLINO: Similar to Sambuca, but with a rougher taste: better to use in cooking rather than drinking.

SAVOIARDI BISCUITS: Italian sponge biscuits widely used in desserts like tiramisù.

CONVERSION TABLES

The following amounts have been rounded up or down for convenience. All have been kitchen tested.

METRIC TO IMPERIAL

10-15g	½oz
20g	¾oz
30g	1oz
40g	1½oz
50-60g	2oz
75-85g	3oz
100g	3½oz
125g	4oz
150g	5oz
175g	6oz
200g	7oz
225g	8oz
250g	9oz
300g	10½oz
350g	12oz
400g	14oz
450g	1lb
500g	1lb 2oz
600g	1lb 5oz
750g	1lb 10oz
1kg	2lb 3oz

50-55ml	2fl oz
75ml	3fl oz
100ml	3½fl oz
120ml	4fl oz
150ml	5fl oz
170ml	6fl oz
200ml	7fl oz
225ml	8fl oz
250ml	8½fl oz
300ml	10fl oz
400ml	13fl oz
500ml	17fl oz
600ml	20fl oz
750ml	25fl oz
1 litre	34fl oz

Please note:
a pint in the UK is 16fl oz
a pint in the USA is 20fl oz

OVEN TEMPERATURES

Celsius	Fahrenheit	Gas Mark
120°	250°	1
150°	300°	2
160°	325°	3
180°	350°	4
190°	375°	5
200°	400°	6
220°	425°	7

BAKING TIN SIZES

Common square and rectangular baking pan sizes:

20x20cm	8x8 inch
23x23cm	9x9 inch
23x13cm	9x5 inch loaf pan/tin

Common round baking pan sizes:

20cm	8 inch
23cm	9 inch
25cm	10 inch

Note also baking paper = non-stick baking parchment.

In New Zealand, South Africa, the UK and the USA 1 tablespoon equals 15ml. In Australia 1 tablespoon equals 20ml.

Walnut Biscuits with Caramelised Kernels - see recipe on page 83

INDEX

These symbols indicate: O Dairy free recipe □ Wheat-free recipe

ACKNOWLEDGEMENTS

My warmest thanks to Renée Lang, who followed this book from conception to end.
Thanks to my beautiful models, in alphabetical order:
Arantxa, Brigitte, Emilia, Lily, Matthew, Max, Nicola and Yana.
Tableware: Milly's Kitchen Shop; Via Emilia; author's private collection.
Author's clothes: Doriana Italian Boutique.

Ciambella alla Ricotta – see recipe on page 13